Cultivating God's Garden through Lent

Cultivating God's Garden through Lent

Margaret Rose Realy, Obl. O.S.B.

Patheos Press | Englewood, CO

1st edition
Published by Patheos Press
Englewood, Colorado

12 13 14 15 16 17 18 19 20 21 – 10 9 8 7 6 5 4 3 2 1

This book uses the New American Bible, Revised Edition, World Catholic Press, 2011.

Cover design by Shatter

Library of Congress Cataloging-in-Publication Data

Realy, Margaret Rose.
    Cultivating God's Garden through Lent.
    ISBN 978-1-939221-09-4

PRINTED IN THE UNITED STATES OF AMERICA

For information, contact Patheos Press, 383 Inverness Parkway, Suite 260, Englewood CO 80112, or contact us online at
www.patheos.com/Books/Patheos-Press.

Contents

Introduction

Crawling out the upstairs window as a kid, I would scramble across the back side of the laundry-room roof. From there I would swing up into the large and sprawling pear tree that grew between the house and the shed, and maneuver between branches to my favorite perch. From my roost I could look into glass greenhouses. The football mums growing inside reminded me of sugar-dot candy on strips of paper. Sitting braced between limbs I watched everything from tiny ants pinching pieces of fruit to semi trucks coughing smoke as they traveled on the five-lane road half a city block away.

Sitting in a pear tree, running through the family greenhouses, squatting to look at miniature flowering buttercups, or lying on my belly watching tadpoles swim in a woodlot pond, I was a child captivated by the Creator's world.

Growing up I lived near 8 Mile and Woodward, a mile and a half outside Detroit. I was surrounded by cement and steel, railroad tracks, loud trucks, and skinny dogs. I listened to the sounds of tanks rolling down Woodward Avenue when the race riots broke out in 1967, listened to the horror of three assassinations on television, and heard the angry male voices that pierced my world. It was hard to imagine a God in all that, let alone listen for His gentle voice.

Still I knew there was something special about roots and shoots, centipedes and chickadees. It was a secret I kept hidden in case somebody would steal it away. As a child I believed that God must have liked me a lot to have put so many things to bring me joy in a world so hard and loud.

We all leave childhood behind and take with us the essence of who we are. For me that essence was a love of plants and little living things, a love that included a fascination with clouds, trees, rivers, and rocks. All this was inextricably entangled with God. To a child's mind, there was no way to distinguish the two; God was nature. He created it not only for our pleasure but to guide us in discerning His presence as the Creator, and the giver of all good things found in creation.

The twelfth-century mystic, healer, and philosopher Hildegard von Bingen created the word *Veriditas* to describe her vision of the greening power of nature, the divine force of God within all life. This "greening of the mind" was the growth of intelligence and spiritual insight through understanding nature's palpable vitality and humankind's discernment of God. The reflections presented in this book are a personal *veriditas*, my attempts of discerning the Creator through His creation.

My hope is that while reading these daily reflections through the forty days of Lent, you will be encouraged to look at the simplicity of the presence of God in nature, and that you will be able to slow down enough, to draw close enough, to hear Him as He whispers.

Opening Prayer

Holy God, Beloved Creator,

As I begin this holy and profound journey through the season of Lent, help me to be always mindful and aware of your presence. Let me clearly see the right path. Help me, Lord, to hear you in the whisper of your creation and to recognize your gift of life complete in the tiniest of seeds.

I draw closer and am filled by you through daily observances that empty me of my self, allowing a refocus on the needs of others. Through the lengthening of days that bring me to Easter, let me grow in joy as I grow nearer to you.

Amen.

Ash Wednesday to First Sunday of Lent

Seeking Growth

You and I are readying ourselves to begin the journey of Lent. Whether it is our first time or our fiftieth, our intent is to grow more fully with God as we move through life toward our eternity.

Ash Wednesday is unique in that as Catholics we begin this season of new life with the full awareness of death. We are told, "you are dust and unto dust you will return." The ashes crossed on our foreheads are made from last year's dried out palm tree leaves, or fronds. The fronds are burnt and transformed for a new purpose—to be the symbolic mark of our death, the threshold through which a heavenly eternity is made possible by the Cross of Christ and his resurrection.

We are reminded by this sacramental act that all is transition away from our brief life. We bear the reminder and publicly acknowledge that we are God's, and that we are willing to be his children, to learn the lessons of being part of this family. We are reminded that being part of a family often means surrendering our wants and walking beside the footprints of Jesus, giving of ourselves.

In seeking to grow spiritually we learn to rely on God. We fast from and let go of unnecessary wants. In letting go we free ourselves to be open, to reach toward God for and in our needs. We give of ourselves in prayer and in acts of charity. In all this we persevere in setting roots that grow beyond the shifting sands of earthly life.

This chapter begins a Lenten journey of spiritual growth. Starting these reflections on Ash Wednesday, we start a habit of drawing closer to God. Researchers tell us that a new habit becomes part of our lives if practiced for thirty days. How much more secure can we become in forty?

Ash Wednesday

Fasting from...

I like the season of Lent, a time to reset my balance point. It is a spiritual time for fresh seeds and new growth. The word Lent is derived from Old English *lencten,* which means "lengthen" and refers to the increase of daylight hours. It is a period of transition from late winter to early spring...the time of developing roots.

When I returned to the Church as an adult, Lent took on a new definition from what I had been taught as a child. I no longer saw Lent as a time for suffering through meatless Fridays and weeks without candy, or attending solemn church services under the dedicated watch of habited nuns.

I'm not a catechist who teaches about the Church, and I don't know all the formal rules and fancy words for this liturgical season. What I do know is that it is a time to practice prayer and charity, offering up to Our Lord little bits of myself.

Like many Christians, I give up something during Lent. I don't remember exactly when the concept took hold, but at some point I chose to *do* something rather than *not* do something. One year during a late winter retreat a small handout was distributed and the idea of "giving up," or fasting, took on a whole new purpose. Here is what it said:

Fast from bitterness; turn to forgiveness
Fast from hatred; return good for evil
Fast from negativism; be positive
Fast from complaining; be grateful
Fast from pessimism; be an optimist
Fast from harsh judgments; think kindly thoughts
Fast from worry; trust in Divine Providence
Fast from discouragement; be full of hope
Fast from anger; be more patient

Fast from pettiness; be more mature
Fast from gloom; enjoy the beauty around you
Fast from jealousy; pray for trust
Fast from gossiping; control your thoughts
Fast from sin; turn to virtue

Maybe I should consider hanging this list on the fridge for more than the forty days of Lent.

"It is our emptiness and trust that God needs, not our plentitude."

~D. Boyland, OCSO

Thursday after Ash Wednesday

Fast from bitterness; turn to forgiveness
Fast from hatred; return good for evil

It was a relatively small patch that I had dug at the back end of the yard to the rental house where I planned a vegetable garden. As an undergraduate at MSU, and a decade older than my classmates, I knew that growing my own food was a necessity; I did not have parents supporting my education.

I dug a portion of the sod and broke up clumps, picked stones and broken glass from the soil, raked it smooth, and mounded the edges to help direct water. Purchasing seeds, I then planted the early season crops of peas, radishes, kales, and a few herbs. A few weeks later I would purchase starter plants for vegetables that took longer to mature such as eggplants, tomatoes, and peppers.

I returned home rather late after classes one day about a week later and again headed to the back of the yard to water the seedlings before sunset. A few feet away I stopped dead in my tracks, saddened by the state of my garden patch. The mounded edges had been kicked into the lawn. Two-thirds of the patch had been covered over with pieces of hand-dug sod, while the remaining third was trampled. Apparently I had unknowingly encroached into the neighbor's property.

Disheartened, I cleaned up what remained but knew I did not have enough time in my schedule to expand the now even smaller patch.

Soon afterwards, as weather permitted, I planted starters of tomatoes and eggplants in the remaining section of garden. In another garden area bordering the house I tucked in some bush zucchini seeds.

Throughout the summer when I was studying in my room, I would often hear the neighbor mowing his yard and anxiously hoped my plants were safe. They were often coated with grass clippings but never really damaged.

It wasn't long until the fruits of my labor ripened and canning and freezing commenced. There is something about tomato and zucchini plants in that I always underestimate their production. Even with the smaller plot I had an overabundance.

While washing the vegetables I looked out the window over the kitchen sink. Sitting in the shade of a large sycamore tree was the woman who lived with the man who mowed the lawn that covered my plants with debris. What I saw was just another woman on a hot August day trying to find a cool place to sit. I had lived next to her for almost a year and never knew her name. After all, I was just another student in the rental house next door.

I carefully laid newspapers in the bottom and up the sides of a small cardboard box. I placed a few small zucchini to one side and then piled several large tomatoes on the other. I took a deep breath and headed out the screened side door.

As I approached the woman I introduced myself and held out the box of vegetables. I could tell by the look on her face she was surprised to see me. I think she realized for the first time that I, the student next door, was close to her own age and not a teenager.

As she accepted my gift she seemed dumbfounded by my presence. She never rose from the lawn chair or told me her name. Avoiding eye contact, she spoke a barely audible "Thanks."

Feeling rejected, but without bitterness, I turned away and went back to my kitchen to continue putting food by. Looking again through the window I noticed that my neighbor had left her shady area and taken with her my gift.

That September I found a room in a house closer to campus. Before I moved away I kicked the mounded edges of dirt into the little patch that had been my garden, smoothed it over, and dusted it with seeds for new lawn. I patted down my pant legs and "shook the dust from my sandals," knowing I had already moved on.

Heavenly Father,

Guide me to always reflect you to those around me. Spare me the shame of reciprocal behaviors rooted in personal pride and let me not limit your love to human love. Grant me to be charitable and forgiving in the face of apathy or anger, so that those whom I meet will know it is you that I serve.

Amen.

Friday after Ash Wednesday

Fast from negativism; be positive
Fast from complaining; be grateful

The piece of ground on which I planned to work was choked with weeds, riddled with tangled bramble roots, and armored by canes of wild roses. Small boulders and saplings warned me of the challenges ahead. This unused piece of land, a wilderness consuming two-thirds of my city lot outside Detroit, was set in my mind to flourish and be fruitful.

I began to dig. I dug with determination and a sense of hope and joy in my heart. I buried all the comments about the impossibility of my endeavor. A song in my spirit shored me up for the work that lay ahead.

For there, just below the surface, beyond the boulders, brambles, roses, and roots lay a soil teeming with life and possibilities. I needed only to find my way in.

I found my systematic approach to clearing the land gradually bending. The reclamation plan of "doing A then B" soon gave way to the functionality of focusing on working one small area at a time and slowly moving into the next tangled mess.

Arduously I labored. Every shovel thrust seemed to meet with resistance from embedded rocks hidden beneath the soil. Every sapling seemed to have a root system that belied its small stature. As I unearthed obstructions I was surprised by the amount of glass and rubbish that was also buried there. What I had thought to be uncontaminated land turned out to be somebody's dumping ground; the weeds merely hid their sins.

It wasn't long before I had mounds of limbs and roots to burn. The stones had been carted off with larger rocks rolled to the side. The granite boulders were part of this land and would remain. Now exposed, they offered a foundational beauty. The weeds that had been piled in an out-of-the-way location were beginning to break down and would in time compost enough to be nourishment for the soil from which they were removed. The old bicycle tires, plastics, and glass rubbish had been bagged and discarded.

Eventually the little piece of land, my backyard, was cleared and the smooth dark soil lay soft and clean. It had been resurrected and was ready for new life. It would now serve a purpose of fruitfulness and beauty. I would lovingly attend to the dwarf fruit trees soon to be planted and the flowers and herbs that would accompany them through the seasons. I was grateful for the gift of perseverance.

"...perform good works all the days of your life, and do not tread the path of wrongdoing. For if you are steadfast in your service, your good works will bring success...."

(Tobit 4:5-6)

Saturday after Ash Wednesday

Fast from pessimism; be an optimist
Fast from harsh judgments; think kindly thoughts

I had secured a work-study job cleaning and washing glassware for a lab in the Botany and Plant Pathology Department at Michigan State University. I had changed majors from horticulture because I couldn't keep up with the class load and work requirements. Botany and plant pathology offered me a way to continue to work with plants and incorporate a growing awareness of my being a systems type of person.

It didn't take long for the graduate students and professors on that floor to realize I did not fit in. I was from a depraved metropolitan area, had not attended high school, and did not have the necessary foundations for research. I was also not good at small talk and usually remained silent rather than bumble my way through luncheon conversations.

I was judged, at times harshly and often for good reason. I didn't have the exposure to sciences and mathematics that the younger students, fresh from high school, had acquired. One particularly painful event took place while a graduate student was doing research utilizing dry ice. I had never seen dry ice before and asked about it. He did not hesitate to tell me that he thought I was being coy and my question was ridiculous.

Like most people I too wanted to feel that I was contributing in some small way. I had worked within the labs for over a year and asked the professor and aforementioned grad student if I could do something besides wash beakers and centrifuge tubes...like maybe learn about their research. They decided to let me run a test of growth hormones on seedlings. I was excited and asked for instructions on how to proceed. When asked if I knew how to grow seeds—and of course as a gardener I did—I answered yes. They then handed me a small brown bag of seeds and multiple bottles with mixing directions and said, "Then just go and do it."

For months I carefully tended, measured, and recorded the progress of my seedlings, delighted to think I was part of a research team. The morning after the study ended, I confidently turned in my results, only to be mocked during lunch. The study was flawed from the start. I was simple and ignorant of the research protocol that they knew so well, and they had just proved to me and the rest of the staff how ignorant I really was.

I left the program. I was no longer optimistic about a future that would revolve around plants.

It was easy to judge them as harshly as they had judged me. It was easy to be self-defeating and a pessimist. It meant I didn't have to try anymore. Failure was unavoidable, so why make an effort?

I didn't take classes during that summer's break. As I puttered about the yard of the rental house near campus, I eventually came to realize my true nature. I was by birth a gardener with grubby hands and dirty knees, not a scientist. The Botany Department's assessment of me was overly harsh but still contained a kernel of truth. I sincerely hoped they would succeed in their research, which would benefit so many people.

And I would succeed as a gardener. For we are optimists, those of us who plant a seed.

"In the coming world, they will not ask me, 'Why were you not like Moses?' They will ask me, 'Why were you not Zusha?'"

~Rabbi Meshulam Zusha (Zusya)

First Sunday of Lent

Fast from anger; be more patient
Fast from pettiness; be more mature

When I was in my early twenties I was always angry about something. It was the age at which I learned that the world did not revolve around my expectations, and that my constant complaining and pettiness were unproductive.

I was married at eighteen to a man only a year older. It was a good Catholic wedding with fourteen attendants, the officiating priest a relative, and the nave of the church filled to capacity with extended family and the friends of our parents.

It was 1972 and in keeping with the theme of that era, I had wanted to be married in a garden wearing a ring of flowers on my head and a gauzy white gown that I would make myself. I had imagined a small gathering of well-wishers with a porch reception of cake and tea.

My very Catholic grandmother and mother would hear none of it. There would be a three-tiered veil instead of the halo of flowers on my long blonde hair. The small wedding I desired — one that would not put everyone into debt — remained a fantasy.

The ceremony, reception, honeymoon, and following two years were relatively uneventful. It was in the third year of this marriage when the starry-eyed love wore off that I noticed a significant change in my husband. It was not a good change.

He was moody and angry and I often responded the same way, mirroring his behaviors. We became annoyed at the least provocation, petty and controlling in our anger. He was rarely at home.

I was too young and ill-equipped to recognize the root of his behaviors. I often believed him when he said I was the cause of all the marital unrest. That was until the day he left me for my brother's wife.

My anger and pain consumed me.

I was forced to move from the apartment we shared as husband and wife. I was not financially able to support myself, so my brother, who was also reeling from the actions of our spouses, offered to let me share his house. Living with him until I found my footing should have been a blessing for both of us. The problem was that my anger and hurt bled into nearly everything. I would pick away at every emotional wound inflicted by my ex and share my suffering with whoever was at hand. I was impatient with myself and those around me. I tried to make things go the way I wanted them to go. I had lost control of myself and my world.

Eventually people stopped calling to see how I was doing. It took a while but one day I realized that my immature ways of dealing with the hurt and anger had driven them all away, including my brother. Shortly thereafter I moved from his house into our grandmother's home.

It took time and a lot of coaching from my grandmother for me to let go of the anger and learn to be more patient through the healing process. I don't recall any single thing she said as much as I remember the calmness that she encouraged. It was a time of maturing as a woman and recognizing how much my behavior influenced the world around me.

Now, in my late fifties, I continue to learn about patience and occasionally laugh at my own pettiness when things do not meet my expectations. Some days it's a challenge to be charitable in all things. But to be charitable is my personal definition of maturity.

"Do not look forward to the mishaps of this life with anxiety…Do not think about what will happen tomorrow, for the same eternal Father who takes care of you today will look out for you tomorrow and always. Either he will keep you from evil or he will give you invincible courage to endure it. Remain in peace; rid your imagination of whatever troubles you."

~St. Francis de Sales

First Week of Lent

The Creator's Joyful Gifts

The Creator's gift to us of experiencing a taste of heaven's joy can be found in the ordinariness of our daily lives. Finding God in the simple things of life draws our attention to His nearness and helps transform our perceptions of what it is to believe and have faith.

We are spiritually nourished in the process of seeking Him, but we must actively search. A purposeful quest for God opens our hearts and allows us to delight in the movements of His Holy Spirit. But we must be attentive and observant.

Many times I have doubted God's timing. Praying intently on issues that I faced, I would wonder not so much if I was being heard but why I couldn't perceive His answer. Eventually I would experience a change in my heart, if not my circumstances. Over the years I've come to understand that life-changing events, or even lesser situations, would not have been as clearly understood, or as fully valued, if they had come at any other time. To appreciate heaven on earth, you first need to know what earthly life isn't, and this realization too takes time.

God's timing is always perfect when it comes to revealing Himself to us. We must be open and available in the moment and the resulting joy of heaven transforms into happiness on earth.

Monday: Seeking Food

I like to feed the birds, and consequently the mice, deer, and squirrels benefit.

On one occasion in mid-January, a light snow had been falling most of the day. The birds were hungry for suet and sunflower seeds to keep them warm. Pulling my boots on over the top of my plaid flannel pants and slipping into an old hooded sweatshirt, I trudged through the snow, joyfully obliging them by filling the feeders. The grateful black-capped chickadees darted about near my hands, trying to steal a bite before I'd had a chance to finish the job.

Back in the house and sitting in the front room I watched the coppery fox squirrel as it hopped across the snow in my neighbor's yard. It climbed the utility pole and deftly walked across the wire over the busy road. Making a ninety-degree turn, it followed the wire across my yard to the stately white pine and made a short leap into its boughs. I knew it was heading for the fresh supply of seed.

I'd decided during the previous week to stop fussing over the squirrels that visited my avian buffet; I'm sure Saint Francis was proud of me. Instead, I'd stopped at the feed store and picked up some corn and peanuts for the frisky visitors. From the shed I rummaged a large saucer feeder and its chain, hung it about six feet away from the bird feeders, filled it, and waited for my furry friends to find it. It was bewildering to me that, over a week later, the corn and peanuts were still relatively untouched. Only the blue jays visited the saucer, stealing peanuts and littering the snow with hollowed shells.

I watched as the squirrel dropped from the pine boughs and tottered across the stockade fence. It leapt down into a smaller evergreen, scurried under the bird feeders to another shrub, wiggled its way up between the branches, hopped on the window sill, and with a determined leap, hurled itself on the thistle feeder. With one more little hop it reached the final destination and landed on top of the feeder with sunflower seeds.

This was its routine, a well-known course to acquire a few morsels of food. It had habitually followed this path and never looked off to the side where a much more nourishing feast awaited.

A more filling bounty is so close. It lies just beyond the meager bits of gratification found in the routine of daily life. All that is needed is to break a habit and go beyond what is so familiar.

"To live is to change, and to be perfect is to have changed often."

~John Henry Newman

Tuesday: A Breezy Day

The wind is a strong and steady breeze and at times gusts to a moderate gale. It's June and the trees have an entire canopy of leaves that catch the full force of the wind. Their limbs shudder and bend with each assault. The weaker branches have broken off and smaller ones roll across the ground. My grandmother would call a day like this "busy"; everything is in motion.

I love the way the trees move and sway. The larger conifers at the back of my neighbor's yard move in a rocking motion like the elderly at a wedding, their heads swaying back and forth, with bodies still and stable. The movement of the nearby Honey Locust, with its multiple narrow half-inch leaves, creates a smooth and whipping motion. It reminds me of a young girl's hair as she races by on horseback.

There are a lot of things racing by. The bright red petals of the poppies detach from their stalks and flame across the lawn. The small dried flowers of the lilac pepper the air so that you can't tell the difference between them and the sudden spray of sand chafing your face. And the paper litter from the neighbor's yard races with the cars driving down the road.

Most of the smaller birds are hiding in the shrubs, clasping onto branches for dear life. Even the brave and defiant hummingbirds that venture out are flying low. A few birds—the grackles and robins—shoot across the sky like unguided rockets, a tumble of wings and feathers.

Higher up, above the treetops, the larger birds brave the forceful currents more skillfully. They face into the wind, swooping and ascending with wings extended and feathers spread wide. Managing the fullness of each new gust, they glide in a dance with an invisible partner. I imagine that if beaks could smile, theirs would in utter joy.

The wind, like the Will of God, can carry us aloft. We learn how to float in a dance with our divine partner, and sometimes we hold fast to the Lord when the currents of the Spirit are beyond our human understanding. But when we gain the confidence to embrace God's Will, our lives will seem like a grace-filled waltz. And oh, how we can rejoice in that powerful holy dance. Swooping and ascending like the angels, we are caught up in the movement and presence of our God.

"...O Lord and lover of souls...your imperishable Spirit is in all things!"

(Wisdom 11:26, 12:1)

Wednesday: Unexpected Warmth

Leaning against the dented aluminum siding near the back door were snow shovels and a covered pail of deicer. They had replaced the garden spade and rake. It was the beginning of January, and here in the upper Midwest it's usually bitter cold and often covered with snow and ice. Last week Christmas was white and offered familiar images often seen on seasonal cards. The snow glistened in the sun and at night sparkled with colors from decorative outdoor lights. In the rural areas that surround my home, the fields glowed with the light from the moon.

Winter moved in as it always does. The plants go dormant and my immediate world slows and I become quieter. It is a peace-filled time after the bustle of Christmas. It is the time of year when I draw down and snuggle into a nest of pillows. Wrapped in an afghan I read, pray, reflect, and imagine.

This year appeared to be no different. Six inches of snow had fallen two days ago, adding a fresh layer to the existing three. The new snow framed the crèche of the outdoor nativity, my inheritance from my grandmother's garage. Outside my window the birds were perched on the Serviceberry's branches near the feeders, with their feathers puffed up and little heads drawn down.

Today, though, was unusual for winter. The steady rain occasionally worked itself into a downpour. It wasn't a freezing rain but one that thawed. It was nearly fifty degrees outside. Rivulets of water grew into large flowing puddles as the snow and ice melted, flooding the road and ditches. It was also the first time I had experienced a thunderstorm on New Year's Day. It was a turbulent and forceful storm, the garden-chimes dancing and jerking with each gust.

The second day after the rains and warm temperatures, the lawn and Creeping Veronica showed green instead of their depleted winter tan. Even the cardinals and finches were singing. It was an unexpected gift creating a hope-filled feeling of spring.

I sensed awkwardness about this feeling—a falseness—and recognized it as fleeting joy. This unusual warm spell was an event out of sync; it brought short-term happiness that was not in balance with nature. It was not the appropriate time for the gift of spring. The truth was that this aberrant weather could cause more harm than good by encouraging sap to flow and buds to set, too tender to survive the impending cold to come.

I recalled times in my life where immediate gratification did not bring a continuing happiness. Those events too were a gift out of season, often bearing false hope. And on occasions when impulsiveness trumped clarity of thought, they did more harm than good.

There is a lasting joy in waiting and in hoping for a gift in due season. Timing matters, and the timing that matters most is God's timing. I recognized the masquerade of those past few days for what they were: a foreshadowing of what was to come and not the true event that it pretended to be.

I love spring with all of its new life and developing growth. I appreciate it even more after a long winter of rest.

"At Christmas I no more desire a rose
Than wish a snow in May's newfangled mirth;
But like of each thing that in season grows."

~William Shakespeare, *Love's Labour's Lost*

Thursday: The Lord's Candlestick

I don't like being wounded in the garden. I get annoyed when I give gentle loving care to my herbaceous buddies and they assault me.

I am often impaled by certain plants in the garden and try to give them a wide berth when pulling weeds. Roses are the worst offenders and only earn my graces and a place in the garden if they are sturdy and disease resistant. Black raspberry bushes are another, and only tolerated because of their fruit.

The one assailant that I'd often forget about was the Yucca, also known as The Lord's Candlestick. In rural Appalachia they are regionally known as "meat hangers" for a very good reason. The tough fibrous leaves with their sharp tips were used to puncture meat and then knotted to form a loop with which to hang the meat for curing in smoke houses.

More than once I yelped when my bare legs were pricked by the Yucca's pointy tipped leaves. On one occasion while mowing, I had been wounded once too often by a plant located near the edge of the lawn. Retaliation was meted out with a saw and spade, and the plant remained shriveling in the middle of the drive for weeks!

I love the architectural beauty of Yucca plants and their striking four- to five-foot stalks of creamy-white flowers. I had come to appreciate these handsome plants on a deeper level one day in early August, the month in which the feast of the Transfiguration of Christ is observed.

It had been a cool summer and most of the perennials were flowering later than usual. I was cleaning up a small bed along the driveway and gingerly pulling the neighbor's intrusive blue-flowering vinca vine from between rose canes and lance-shaped leaves of the Yucca. Like most gardeners while working in a garden, I think about life or pray for those who come to mind. Often I have a note-pad and pen nearby for those God moments of inspiration that lead to later reflection — as this story did.

Kneeling on a pad in the driveway, I reached in repeatedly to remove the vine from between the Yucca leaves. Absentmindedly I stabbed my arm on one of the tips. I pulled back with a low murmur of pain, looked up at the massive flowering stalk and intended to have a short disgruntled conversation with God. Instead He decided to have a moment with me.

There, three feet over my head, against a clear, bright-blue sky was a glowing white oblong shape of flowers. I imagined I could almost see Jesus wearing his luminous white robes in the Transfiguration as it was told in the Bible. I was captivated, not unlike the apostles, I'm sure.

The incongruity of the radiant flowers rising from the earthly whorl of piercing lance-shaped leaves reminded me of Jesus' brief life. How his presence was wholly incongruent with this world. How he too would be pierced, and by a lance, and would rise past the violence and pain.

Through all this — the Transfiguration and The Passion — we were shown by Our Lord a way to be "of God" and not just for God. We were shown how to live in a world of piercing sharpness that is discordant and not in harmony with the soul's desire to be illuminated and illuminating.

I studied the Yucca for a moment longer knowing my soul had become a little brighter from the small revelation. I knew on that day I would never see the Yucca in the same way again and never have.

Intending to return to my task of clearing vinca from the lance shaped leaves I noticed the flowering stalk was shading my face; a nice touch to end the lesson. The transfigured Jesus stands between me and the hot-white light of God. I reached for my notepad and pen, captivated again.

"Be attentive to the Word
As to a lamp shining in a dark place
Until day dawns
And the morning star rises in your heart."

(Psalms 33:1-9)

Friday: Attentiveness to Details

The big Eastern White Pine tree that grew at the southwest corner of the house was recently removed by the local power company.

When it was young, I would attach food to it during the winter to feed the animals: peanut butter-coated pinecones rolled in seed, corn cob halves hung with twine, and home-baked animal cookies full of protein. Its adolescent boughs held out hope for many animals when food was scarce.

As it grew, the boughs spread further into the garden. It wasn't until many years later that I figured out it was not the cultivar I had thought it to be. This Eastern White Pine was going to be big, very big. It had not been planted in an appropriate site so as to grow to its full potential.

So it grew, as the cliché goes, "where it was planted." It protected the birds, housed the squirrels, and hid the raccoons. It buffeted winter winds and provided shade from hot summer suns.

I would listen from my upper bedroom windows as its boughs whispered when the winds blew through them. When working in the yard I would often stop and touch its long delicately soft needles, the same needles that would fall off in late summer and provide beautiful golden mulch for the flower beds. I loved how the new growth, called candles, would come out pointing toward heaven, and how the pollen would burst into the air like incense when I thumped the male cone clusters with my hand.

Repeatedly it needed harsh pruning to keep its limbs off the house. The lower boughs encroached into the yard so far that they eventually had to be trimmed up the trunk so one could walk under them. Its expansive limbs grew between the electrical wires and were repeatedly trimmed back by the power company. With all this cutting-back as it grew it became misshapen, less beautiful than it was intended to be.

Yet it was as fully what it could be in the circumstances in which it was planted.

During storms, and there are many of them here, the branches would hit the wires as well as the sides of the house. During one particularly nasty winter, three massive limbs broke off due to snow loads. The blessing was that they brushed against and then fell free of the power lines, and completely missed the house and wooden stockade fence.

I had prayed many times about that tree. It needed to be removed and I could not pay to have that done. It was ruining the siding of the house. It was a threat to my neighbors during the winter because of its potential to create a power outage. It grew only feet from my bedroom wall and I feared a wind shear or tornado would drive it through the roof. I loved that tree. I was also frightened by it.

My prayers were answered one spring day when a representative from a tree trimming service hired by the power company came to my door. The young man who stood there very respectfully explained about the neighborhood pruning that would take place in a few weeks. As I walked outside with him, he delicately tried to describe to me what this large, already misshaped pine would look like if they trimmed it back the required distance to free the power lines.

While he spoke I was secretly hoping that the Holy Spirit had moved someone somewhere to answer my earlier prayers. When he asked permission to completely remove the tree I nearly squealed. He looked at me, startled and a little relieved as I exuberantly answered, "Oh yes, please!"

Having an overgrown tree removed may not seem like suitable stuff for prayers, especially when I think about a friend dying of cancer or the violence in the world. Yet, there it is once again, God's attentiveness to the smallest details in my life. I sometimes think God just wants to see me wriggling with delight.

My Lord,

Let me always be confident in your love. Help me to know in my heart that every prayer uttered, no matter how seemingly insignificant, is heard by you. Let us accept that the betterment of a soul is always your answer to prayer, and be assured that you are ever present in the details of our lives.

Amen.

Saturday: Fragrant Memories

Each spring when the air is rich with fragrance I am taken back to days of wonder when I ambled alone through my childhood neighborhood just outside Detroit. As a youth I was fascinated by the natural world. Even in an environment of blacktop and tar, nature still persisted.

It seemed every block I would walk down had at least one lilac bush in lavender, white, or dark reddish-purple. Most of the mothers in the neighborhood with this shrub in their yard would have a Mason jar spilling over with cut blooms on the kitchen table, perfuming the house.

One yard along Martin Road had a lovely and strongly perfumed white flowering shrub, which as an adult I learned was a *Viburnum burkwoodii*. It flowered just before the lilacs and its scent was so strong in the mornings that I could enjoy it from several blocks away. I'm sure the elderly woman who lived there thought it strange that I, a little girl, would keep walking back and forth in front of her house, lifting my arms like a slow-moving bird so I could breathe deeper the sweet scent of spring.

Many scents evoke childhood moments of delight. There was the heady odor from wasteland ponds coming back to life, and I knew that soon pollywogs would be skimming the edges of the murky water. There was the tickling smell of grass being mowed and the rich musty scent of blackcurrant bushes with yellow flowers that mimicked forsythias. With my head tipped back I would often follow my nose, deeply drawing in a scent as I tried to find its source.

Other smells stir my heart. The smell of fresh dill still carries me back to my grandmother's kitchen and when we would pickle hot dilled green tomatoes. I'm always mindful to plant this herb in with my perennials. Each time I rub against it I think of my grandmother, after whom I am named, and who nurtured my love of gardening. She and I would also make hundreds of jars of jellies and jams for Christmas gifting. The aroma from black raspberries reducing for jelly would cling to my clothes for hours after we had finished waxing the jars.

There are two distinct fragrances that stir my memory of being loved. On my grandmother's dresser there was always a round pink box of Chantilly dusting powder. In a memory box I have a small piece of cloth salvaged from her favorite sundress, cut up for quilting, that still carries her delicate fragrance. The other memory is of her husband, my grandfather, whom we called Buddy. He was a barrel-chested Irishman with an unflappable joy and love affair with life. When I was a child he would nab and lift me by my waist, announcing to the world "It's the Margaret Rose!" as I squealed and giggled, being hugged close to his neck and deeply inhaling his Old Spice cologne.

Scent is a wondrous thing, a curious gift from God. He gave us many gifts through which to find joy and pleasure. The sense of smell is only one, but it was the first of my senses that I realized as a child brought me delight independent of the city around me. Scent cannot be dreamed or imagined. It startles us into the present and in the same moment can carry us adrift into memories of heaven on earth.

"Listen, my faithful children: open up your petals,
like roses planted near running waters;
Send up the sweet odor of incense, break forth in blossoms like the lily.
Raise your voice in a chorus of praise:
bless the LORD for all his works!"

(Sirach 39:13-14)

Second Sunday of Lent: Great White Egret

From childhood and for most of my life I had been a morning person. Rising early I would soon be out the door to greet the day. Whether going to a job, tending the gardens, or walking my dogs, I was a bundle of energy.

That's not so true anymore. The youthful Suzie-Sunshine no longer lives in this body, being replaced by the more determined Little Switch Engine pulling a load uphill. I need time to get myself moving physically and mentally.

One day when I had an appointment, it took effort to rise early. On the road, the morning drive was familiar; four miles past farms, misty swamps and a river, to the stop at the four corners, turn left and straight on into town through the breaking dawn. I was still feeling pretty sluggish; the coffee's caffeine hadn't kicked in yet. My usual morning routine was hampered and I felt off balance attempting to progress into a day started without prayers. With energy level low and bones stiff and aching, I was on automatic pilot and hoping that there would be no need for a sudden cognitive response.

Halfway to town and just before a subdivision are wetlands that I have passed hundreds of times in the past twenty-some years. The marshy area has a clearing next to the road where a small pond exists. Because of its proximity to traffic and people, it is rare to find more than a couple of ducks or geese floating about. Approaching this pond and still at a distance, I couldn't figure out what I was looking at on the water. Whatever it was appeared to be white, unmoving, and completely the wrong shape for swans. Had someone planted white plastic flamingos as a joke?

As I got closer I was startled by what I was seeing standing there. In the crisp morning sun surrounded by a thin rising mist was a flock of Great Egrets, glowing a startling white against the blackish-green of the water. I felt a surge of immense delight at the vision of these fifty-some birds as still as statues, yellow bills perfectly horizontal to the water. I came to a stop (grateful there was no one behind me) and kept whispering, "Oh my God, oh my God..." as I stared at the amazing sight.

It is rare that these birds deviate this far north and west of their summer grounds. With the excessive heat this summer, they apparently thought it warm enough to migrate into our area.

After I had soaked in their beauty, and realizing that several cars had pulled around mine, I continued on to town. I felt exhilarated from the experience—a gift of living and breathing art at the side of a blacktopped two lane road.

God does this in our lives. When we least expect it, and are wholly unprepared, He whispers...and sometimes shouts... "Here! I AM." We are often startled by His nearness when we recognize His hand. Bumbling in amazement and at a loss for words, we experience goose bumps three layers deep. And I think God delights in His delighting us, smiling at our surprise.

"I note the echo that each thing produces as it strikes my soul."

~Unknown

Second Week of Lent

Fruits of the Spirit

The Sunday readings after the Second Week of Lent point toward a change of some kind. We are asked to change in a way to be more of a reflection of God than of our world and to bear the fruit of his Holy Spirit.

When I think of the Fruits of the Spirit I compare them to a prism in the window. When sunlight enters in and bends as it exits, a rainbow becomes visible. But the metaphor here is not about the worn phrase that we are a beautiful rainbow of many hues. The analogy I am going for is that we are the prism in which God bends Himself through us.

Depending on how we are formed by His design or by our rearing, we will change or bend the light of God and manifest him differently as individuals. We split his Light into spiritual colors through faith, hope, and charity or love, the virtues that are infused into our soul. We uniquely express these virtues, gifts and Fruits of the Spirit in subtly different ways.

We are spiritually altered when we become aware that the Light of God is within us. With this awareness, we interact in a new way with the world around us. Those who see and experience this light or fruitfulness in us may also be changed. Through our expression of God, working through us, they may open their hearts to the Light. Once open, they too can learn about and experience the fruits of the Spirit.

It isn't always easy, as Gandhi said, "to be the change you wish to see in the world." But I think God wants us to be fruitful, bringing His Light into a world grown dim.

Monday: Not so Effortless

The annoyances that morning challenged me, and by all indication my attitude needed adjusting.

Before heading for volunteer gardening at the retreat center, nearly an hour's drive away, I needed to fill the car with gas. The pre-pay pumps were rarely an issue, but this time my debit card would not authorize. The scratchy voice from the metal speaker said I needed to come inside to the register.

I had pulled up to Pump-8 at the far end for quick reentry onto the main road. It was, of course, the farthest from the cashier. I trudged the distance and stood in line behind six other customers. The name badge of the woman behind the counter clarified why the wait was so long: Elise was in training.

My exasperation grew when I learned that she didn't know how to override the pump and I would have to pay cash. Money on the counter, I trudged back to the car, filled it, and trudged again to the cashier to wait in line for the change. Heading back across the lot for the fourth time I wondered if I had done my mile walk for the day.

Finally back on the highway and running just a few minutes late, I saw a silver van in my mirrors. It was coming up quickly. When the vehicle, a Dodge Caravan nearly twice the size of my little Ford wagon, was nearly past it suddenly veered into my lane and slowed. I hit the brakes hard, glanced into the rear-view mirror and saw the cars behind me also start to brake. Then my car began to swerve but I quickly regained control. We all nearly collided.

Pulling around the now-slowed Caravan I looked to the driver. She was cluelessly laughing into a cell phone held to her head. Twice in less than a month, while I was on the road, a young woman with a cell had aged me by ten years.

Already behind schedule and knowing I had to pick up items to repair the hoses at the center, I exited the highway and headed for Walmart. Shooting into a parking spot, I dashed into the store as fast as a five-foot full-bodied woman could. I moved quickly to Lawn & Garden, grabbing male and female couplings, washers, plastic hose menders, and shut-offs. Then I headed to one of the only two registers open in the store.

This quick stop wasn't going to be so quick either. I waited with my fewer-than-ten-items behind two other customers as the cashier slowly scanned the groceries of an apparent friend of hers from who-knows-where. The next thing I knew a wailing infant pulled up behind me whose screams were deafening. The poor mother, in pajama bottoms, Crocs, and daddy's t-shirt, looked desperate with a screaming baby in the seat, a whining three-year-old throwing a fit at her side, and a mountainous cart of groceries.

Pity is not a good thing, but I had pity for her, and stepped aside so she would be the next in line. The man in front of me did the same.

Things were not much better when I finally pulled into the retreat center. I was nearly twenty minutes late, which was duly noted by those searching for me on-site. The wheelbarrow had a flat, the tool I needed was at home, and someone had blocked our shelving in the pole barn with bins of oil and tractor parts. Eventually things were sorted out and we all headed out to the gardens. I was grateful to be able to work alone a fair distance from the others.

Not long ago I had read a piece by St. Claude de la Colombriere, a Jesuit priest in the seventeenth century who spoke of turning our hearts to God during the hundred small annoyances we face every day. These aggravations, whether created by others or by ourselves, can train us to face more challenging issues. That morning the reading hit home. The past few hours had not been about mounting an effort for a single heroic virtue. Rather, they were about practicing small charitable acts in the face of exasperation. Somehow I had managed to keep coarse words to myself, my attitude in check, and impatience undetected.

However, I do think I exhibited heroic virtue in not expressing myself symbolically to the driver of the silver Dodge Caravan.

Heavenly Father,

Through all the challenges and unexpected events that meet me in my day, guide me to trust in Your providence. Keep my words, thoughts, and deeds centered on your love that I may always find patience and even humor in the messy circumstances of life.

Amen.

Tuesday: Temperature

Under the apple tree and along the weathered stockade fence grows an established stand of tall Ostrich Plume ferns, *Matteuccia struthiopteris*. They are sometimes called shuttlecock fern because their growth pattern looks very much like a badminton birdie set on its nose. The dramatic single-stemmed fronds rise four feet high out of a central crown and in moist shaded regions of Canada are known to grow up to six feet tall. They spread rapidly by rhizomes, a root system creeping horizontally just below the leaf mulch that sends up new plants. The roots of this fern are sensitive to soil temperature and stop spreading where soil is too warm. In my garden the line of delineation of this invasive fern is remarkable; it has never encroached into full sun.

On the other hand, there are plants that need high soil temperature to begin growth, like the wild Butterfly Weed, *Asclepias tuberosa*. Grown in full sun it rarely shows shoots until midsummer, liking the soil hot and dry. During August in Michigan it flashes with showy orange flowering clusters along roadsides. Butterflies, especially the Monarch, and hummingbirds depend on this late season food source.

The temperature of soil affects root development for different plants depending on their unique characteristics. What about our spiritual temperature and its effect on our soul?

I have at times worried about my spiritual temperature. How do I compare to those white-hot writers who can proclaim God and correlate texts with authority? Where do I fall on the continuum so clearly laid out in the Bible where being lukewarm is vile, and being fervent and boiling over with the Spirit is desired? At what temperature does my soul grow best?

Consider the gifts of the Spirit and how we are all uniquely endowed. Let's start by thinking about boiling points. Different elements boil at different temperatures. Some of us are more fervent, having a low boiling point that allows for an easy bubbling up with controlled intensity. Others, like me, simmer on low and on occasion are moved by the Spirit to rise up, needing to be careful not to boil over at the sudden flame. Not everyone can be, or was designed to be, a crucible of intense fire when the Holy Spirit burns in the soul.

If I am not fervent, am I lukewarm? Are there areas of my life where I am content with just being tepid, especially when it comes to living for Jesus? Tepid is defined as being neither hot nor cold, characterized by a lack of force or enthusiasm. It is a static, apathetic state where there is neither growth nor decline.

A friend of mine loves roses and decided to grow a few on her lovely wooded hillside property. She adamantly maintained that the sparse, infrequently flowering bushes were just fine in the dappled-shade garden in which they were planted. They survived but did not thrive; they were not dead but did not live in a way that would reveal their full beauty. My friend was content with their static state—it was good enough.

When it comes to the tepidity or fervency of a soul, I try to consider the unique characteristics of the individual as equipped by God. Some of us grow more prolifically and bring beauty in less intense environments. Others express beauty in the heat and are able to nourish the faithful when it seems too desperate for the rest of us.

Not everyone can be white-hot in expressing love for God, but we can all keep the burner on.

"When we surrender our lives to God, the light and beauty that shines forth is as effortless as that of a wildflower—it is the work of God's hand alone."

~Anonymous

Wednesday: Fruitfulness

Being a work-study student in the 1980s meant carrying a full class load and working twenty hours weekly for the university I attended. I was awarded this form of financial aid before the Reagan Administration ended the program.

In the summer this included working the university's research arbors and orchards. I loved the opportunity to ride into the countryside on my knobby-tire five-speed bike. With tools, water, and lunch securely tied in the rear wire-baskets, and a straw hat slapping my back, I would ride along farm lanes and down dirt roads that led to the fields.

The orchards of apples and vineyards of grapes were experimental pollen crosses. Once the fruit was collected for research in early autumn, what was left was free for the taking, and so I took. There was a palm-sized apple that I loved best. Coral-colored, firm, sweet and when I bit into it, the apple's juice ran down my arm. It was considered a failure because within forty-eight hours of harvesting it turned soft and flavorless. I would pick and eat a couple of these apples as I worked, tuck a few in a bag for later that night, and repeat the process the next day until they were gone. I was forever after ruined for grocery store apples.

There were days that a graduate student and I would be out in the fields with a professor who was a consummate teacher. He would prattle on about growing trees and vines all the while we were working. I learned more about plants and soils from his casual conversations than I did in any of my classes. One of the lessons was about how a plant absorbs the flavor of the soil in which it grows.

Certain plants demonstrate this trait more than others. The taste of garlic, onions, and grapes are affected by soil composition, especially grapes. Viticulture, the growing of grape vines, is considered a fine art that includes not only pruning, but also the location of the vineyard. Proper soil and land preparation are the keys to successful vine production and the first step toward obtaining good fruit.

If you are "into" wines, you are aware of how region, rainfall, and horticultural practices all affect the taste. Soils vary by region. What is found in California or France is different than that of Michigan or Australia's Hunter Valley. The soils are all suitable to fulfill the needs of the vine, yet each region will produce distinct differences in flavor.

There are similarities here to our fruitfulness, faith, and how we live and grow. God has placed us in different regions and we develop our roots of faith within that "soil." Those of us growing up in rural areas, working cattle or fields of wheat, will express faith differently than someone from New York or Melbourne. We nurture our faith through different people and experiences that add flavor to our expression of belief. Whether we grow up surrounded by reinforced concrete or open range, God's fruit is still sweet and distinctly our own.

"Through [Jesus] let us continually offer God a sacrifice of praise, that is, the fruit of our lips that confess His name. Do not neglect to do good and to share what you have; God is pleased by sacrifices of that kind."

(Hebrews 13:15-16)

Thursday: Garden Apron

The dark tan canvas apron hung in the shed for years.

When the apron was first purchased the ties that crisscrossed the back from the shoulders to around the waist could encompass my middle and tie in front. Many years later I surrendered to being a bit thicker with maturity and tied it in the back.

I was in my twenties when I bought the apron. Thirty-some years ago, the pockets in women's jeans were not deep enough for small tools, and they didn't hold much more than a hankie. Cargo pants were not yet available outside of military issue; and bib-overalls, decorated with peace signs and colorful patches by my peers, were not the look I was going for. The only sturdy aprons available were for roofers, and those pockets too were not suited for carrying garden tools. Searching through commercial clothing catalogs, since there was no Internet then, I eventually found what I needed.

It was an apron not for the faint of heart. The cotton canvas material was thick, stiff, and warm. That was perfect for cool spring or autumn days, but in the heat of summer, rather than wearing the apron I often dragged it across the ground or stretched it between the handles of a wheelbarrow.

I never thought much about that apron until now. It was a tool that was well loved and well used. It held not only pruners, hand saws, knives, and trowels but also assorted sprays for repelling bugs or packages of fertilizers…which often tore open due to the aforementioned tools. The pockets would carry seeds and bulbs for planting in the spring, and handfuls of flower heads collected in the fall.

Each winter when it was too cold to do much in the gardens, the apron would get its yearly laundering. Turning it upside down and holding the straps, I would smack it vigorously against a tree trunk to knock off embedded dirt and free whatever had accumulated deep in the pockets. Once cleaned, it would then do double duty indoors as I attended to household painting and repairs or working with stained glass.

The apron carried more than physical elements for the garden. It also held a gardener's expectation for renewed life, something not easily attained. It takes work and dedication that is fed by love to keep a garden growing and well. Gardeners work and sweat against the elements and with the flow of nature. Over the years we may lose a few battles as when there is a hard freeze late in the season, a drought ensues, or hail storms level what was once beautiful. Picking up our tools, we start again fully accepting the occurrence and trusting in the future.

That garden apron was a visible sign. It was a symbol of a frayed and worn hope—a hope for renewal and a confidence that I could work through whatever befell me.

Eventually after years of service that cotton canvas apron was beyond repair. The pockets were more holes than material and the UV from the sun had weakened what remained of the fiber. One day late in June I cut it into pieces for composting and returned it to the earth…a very fitting end for a well-worn life.

"More things grow in a garden than a gardener sows."

~Spanish Proverb

Friday: Greenhousing

When I was growing up my family's business was a greenhouse that was located a mile and a half outside Detroit in Ferndale. The store front and floral shop was on Hilton Road. On Orchard Street there was about an acre under glass, two city lots of creosote-covered cold frames and three more lots of open field for planting-out. The three family homes were located in-between. At the back of all this, on Lewiston Avenue, was a garage as big as a pole barn and a cement pad for the numerous semi trucks that arrived from late autumn through early summer.

I was a child then and loved the benches of colorful flowers. There was the fall and winter crop of gold-toned cutting mums for floral shops. Next came vibrant red, pink, and white geraniums. The rainbow myriad of annual flats ended the growing season.

Several decades have passed since then. And when the economy plummeted, I lost my job and retuned to my first love, greenhousing. Nothing compares to the clean, humid, oxygenated air found in a plant-filled greenhouse. There is a sense of accomplishment at the end of a growing season when the thousands of flats, seeded up in February, are sold. The customers, grateful for trays of flowers and vegetables, would share with me their hopes for future gardens.

One customer was having problems with plants and asked for my expertise, inviting me to her home. The single glass-framed hothouse was attached off the dining room. Her beautiful collection of common and exotic plants showed minor fungal infections and mites. I made suggestions for resolving these issues, marveled at her collection, and complimented her on her skills. And that was that.

Driving home I realized that the plants she grew were not intended to ever leave the hothouse. They were there for her pleasure and those whom she chose to invite in. I thought about the difference between her and me on the view of the purpose of plants. Each of our collections was no less beautiful than the other's. The difference is that hers stayed put and what I grew went out.

Sharing our faith can be expressed in much the same way: a greenhouse versus a hothouse. In both there is growth, but one, the greenhouse, releases that beauty into the community to develop more fully. We can keep our faith to ourselves only sharing it with those whom we invite in, or we can release it and let it go and grow in our world.

I no longer work greenhouses but fondly remember those years working at Beck's Flowers in Jackson and growing plants that were shared with a clan of gardeners. I like the idea of sharing what I love with others…flowers and faith.

Compassionate and Loving Father,

You have given us a spirit of joy and endowed each of us with a gift through which to share your love. Help me to embrace the uniqueness of my gift allowing me to share the faith more fully with those I meet on this wondrous journey.

Amen.

Saturday: Directional Pruning

I love to prune. It's like art to me, a hope filled art. Each cut is intended to produce either a directional growth, to form and shape hardwoods for beauty, or to enhance the bearing of fruit.

Sometimes with ornamental trees a whole section of limb that rubs against another needs to be removed, allowing the stronger limb to develop more fully. At other times the interior has become so cluttered with unnecessary branches that they block the light from reaching deep inside. More often if pruning has been done regularly, it is a simple nip here or there to keep things growing as they should.

When doing light pruning I look at the bud that would be just behind the cut and estimate its future growth pattern. Will it grow backwards and into the interior? Does it face out and up toward the sun? I imagine and calculate the plant's development before daring to trim it back.

I like to get an overall view of the condition and shape of a tree as I work. On more than one occasion the Groundskeeper at the retreat center where I volunteer has lovingly chided me as I repeatedly circle my object of renovation. Maybe I do take too seriously the ramifications of my pruning efforts. But like other things in my life, I do not want to throw things off balance through carelessness or haste.

I contemplate as I prune on being pruned, or even, as of late, being cut to the ground and starting anew. As I have done with plants, so God too rings-me-round, looking to balance growth. My interior life sometimes becomes overcrowded with things of this world, hampering the light of God from shining in where needed. Other things need to be completely removed so there will be more fruitfulness.

Drawing closer to God in the garden, I come to learn that in His pruning He too wants beneficial maturing, purposefully directed.

"Give me Lord what will rebound to your own profit."

~*Magnificat*

Third Sunday of Lent: The Trees or the Well

It's a hard question for gardeners when there is a severe drought: Do the trees get watered or should the well be saved? Both seem essential to life.

The news report said that the drought in my area mimicked the intensity and duration of the Dust Bowl in the 1930s. It was crippling. Driving the back roads of surrounding counties I saw the crops fail on the family farms of Hannewald, Sweet, and Katz. Their fields of soy and corn were stunted, curled, and dull. I passed by dark black holes that used to be their irrigation ponds, now lined with a cracked layer of dried curled mud.

I noticed the rigidity of the corn stalks. Their desiccated leaves were no longer a supple green, but dull silver and only a day or two away from turning dark tan. They looked pained as their leaves rolled tightly in upon themselves, pointing toward the heavens, a congregation begging in prayer. The final act of violence by this vandal of summer was to lay low the stalks. A stiff breeze blew hot at 104 degrees, and the stalks unable to stand against the searing wind fell to the ground like dominoes, whole fields laid to waste.

The trees were no less devastated; their suffering was just less obvious. The tips of limbs were flaccid, and hanging from them were dull limp leaves curling in. Towards the center of the tree shards of vivid red and yellow leaves clung uselessly by dried-out stems.

Massive oak trees that were seedlings after the last 100 Year Drought were now in decline. Other beautiful mature trees that gave us shelter, shade, and food were also on a slow march toward death. My bright yellow Honeylocust, the aged apple tree, the crabapple, and serviceberry—all needed water. They felt like dear friends who all at once were stricken by the same disaster. So many in need; could I not at least save one?

My heart cried for my trees, for my neighbor's woodlot behind the fence, for the neighborhood wells that had dried up, for the stately evergreens at the retreat center that had sheltered four generations of souls into spiritual development. I faced an obvious but disconcerting choice of who would live from what water remained underground. It is hard for gardeners to resign themselves to the loss of a mature tree whether from disease or drought.

The right choice might have been to conserve water for families and to surrender our own wants for their well-being. Knowing that didn't make the decision any easier. Choosing what is right is not always so obvious, but it is easy to spot absolute truth, wanting what is best for another.

Like the corn stalks, I too raised my arms in supplication for rain. I prayed not only for my neighbors' wells, but also for our trees.

"Growth in selfless love is not natural to fallen human beings. Only the power of God's Spirit and our surrender to it can explain a steady growth in charity."

~R. H. Chabot, *The Death of Atheism*

Third Week of Lent

Illumination

There is a quote by Albert Einstein that says, "When the solution is simple, God is answering." A simple solution, the truth of the matter, illuminates our thoughts and our lives. But getting to the truth is often complicated and muddied by our personal wants for a self-serving answer.

Looking at the truth of our lives, at what we have or have not done, can be a source of anxiety and remorse. When we hold onto things that don't matter we can cause a spiritual blindness to come over us. Wading through our faults takes courage and sometimes the help of others. It is in lifting the blindness that darkens our souls that we become able to see the truth of our God more clearly.

I have found it a challenge to look at things I fear, not only in relation to my world but what I fear or dislike in myself. We all have hidden things, good and bad, but it is in holding onto what we dislike that we stay trapped and choose to remain distanced from Our Father. We deny a simple truth with the relativism of our situations and desires.

What is this truth? That we are children of God, loved by him, and there is nothing we can do to change that...we will always be loved. God attempted to make this obvious to us thick-headed humans centuries ago when he gave his only Son, so that everyone who believes in Him might not perish but might have eternal life. God desired that the world might be saved through Him...and this is the verdict, that light came into the world (John 3:16-19).

The solution is acceptance, believing God's answer that He already loves us. Let us have faith that when we rinse the dirt off our hearts and turn around, we will be illuminated by his Light. We know that we are His and will always be welcomed home.

Monday: Garter Snakes

I pulled at a clump of weedy henbit spreading across the raised wooden soon-to-be vegetable bed. Just inches away from my hand was unexpected movement. Initially startled and inhaling sharply, I pulled back. My miniature pinscher, Lilly, always ready on the defense, came dashing over to see what had made me react so suddenly.

Watching the area for additional movement I noticed two garter snakes slowly slide away. Apparently I had disturbed them as they lay sunning on a bright spring day. I shooed the dog away so she would not harm the pair and sat back on my heels to watch the dull-black snakes move through the recently mowed lawn.

I'm not afraid of garter snakes though at times they may startle. I know many people who are so terrified of them, or any snake, that they run off screaming as fast and as far as they can to get away. Garter snakes are harmless and rather friendly little things to have in the garden. They love to eat slugs, small rodents, bugs, and almost anything that will sate their meaty appetites.

I was surprised the first time I touched one of these garden companions. The little stinker had somehow gotten into the warm house on a cool night in late summer. My housemate, who is afraid of snakes, was of no use. A grown woman, she was upstairs in a panic, screaming like a schoolgirl! I knew these snakes were harmless, but still, picking one up barehanded was a little disconcerting. As the snake began to quickly slither away from me across the basement floor, I grabbed it behind its head. I was surprised at how warm its little body was and how its skin felt smooth and satiny against my arm. What little fear I had of these snakes was dispelled, though I do admit to eagerly depositing it outside the house and thoroughly, and repeatedly, washing my hands.

There is a reading in the Bible in Numbers 21:6-9 that tells of the Israelites being besieged by venomous snakes after cursing God and Moses for their trying situation of wandering in the wilderness. Moses is directed by God to make a bronze snake and place it on a pole so that anyone who looked upon it could be healed from the bites of the snakes. To be healed, they had to look upon the very thing that frightened and harmed them.

Not an easy thing to do, to look at what we fear. A quote by Eleanor Roosevelt is taped to the side of my computer monitor and reads, "You gain strength, courage and confidence by every experience in which you really stop to look fear in the face...You must do the thing which you think you cannot do." At times we must also face the things we think we cannot bear.

Watching the two garter snakes circling back across the sunny stone walkway I noticed their markings. The female's coloring was a soft mossy green, and the male's bright lime; they were a mating pair. Steadily they made their way closer to where I sat and, hesitating for a moment, possibly looking upon me with fear, reentered their den under the wood-framed garden.

I returned to my weeding and realized that seeing fear for what it really is helps me to also see the blessings in being afraid: being blessed with a growing confidence in reacting appropriately, taking lessons of courage into other areas, and gaining mastery over an emotion God has instilled. I'm discovering too how quickly and concisely I can pray in the heat of the moment, a skill most mothers develop in short order.

I also realized that the pair of garter snakes would soon be multiplying their blessings to me in the garden with their babies. I doubt my housemate will ever mow the back lawn again.

"Courage is very important. Like a muscle it's strengthened by use."

~Ruth Gordon

Tuesday: Mammoth Moth

One night about fifteen or so years ago, I saw a moth the size of my hand. Because it was dark, I couldn't get a clear look at its markings, but knew it was the largest moth I had ever encountered. I shared my experience with someone who knew about these sorts of things, who told me it was a Luna moth. And that was the end of that. Until last week.

While watering at the retreat center, I stopped dead in my tracks and slowly turned off the hose. There, on the cement parking bumper, not ten inches from where I stood, was another like the same large moth I had seen ages ago. I assumed it had just hatched because its wings were not fully spread and its fuzzy head was still smooth and flat. It was ever so slowly moving its wings…to which a five-inch spread would be realized.

In my excitement I called to another gardening volunteer who came scurrying over to view my discovery. Then I called over the priests from the retirement community next door, who were out for their morning walks. Momentarily stopping their rosary prayers, they oohed and ahhed at the wondrous sight.

I couldn't contain myself and wanted to share this experience with everyone I could. I called people out of their offices, pulled them from their chores, stopped them as the drove by. We all exclaimed and marveled at the beauty and size of this winged creature.

I knew, from what I had been told years earlier, that seeing one of these moths was amazing in itself. To see one in broad daylight and freshly hatched was truly miraculous! And without hesitation I said so to all who came to see, and told them how privileged we were for the experience, delighted with myself for having recognized the significance of the event.

Eventually we all returned to our tasks, slightly richer for having seen another of the Creator's amazing works.

About two hours later I learned that it was not a Luna moth at all, but a Saturn moth. I felt a deep sense of bewilderment and almost shame for the error I had made. I blindly believed what I was told by someone I thought was an expert. I had spread this false information to others and it felt like I had deceived them into experiencing something that was not true.

What should have remained an awesome experience was now tainted. I was embarrassed and saddened by what should have remained a joy.

To those whom I could, I corrected myself and apologized for misleading them. In my heart I knew I had innocently shared misinformation as "truth," naively perpetuating a falsehood. Graciously, and with minimal disappointment, they each expressed delight in having shared a moment of wonder, no matter what its name.

My lesson in all this is that truth bears out. The truth is that the moth was an amazing creation given to delight us by our God, and that my showing off my presumed knowledge did not add to the beauty of the gift.

"May God deliver us from living in illusion and make us live in truth—the truth of our destiny and the truth of his love and mercy."

~St. Teresa of Avila

Wednesday: Bug Under a Log

It was late in the day and I felt the sun warm my back through the dark green t-shirt. I decided to seek the cool of the shade and continue my weeding there.

The difference of the texture in the soil under the trees was familiar. With all of the fallen leaves the soil was soft and friable with decaying organic material. The weeds pulled out easily without digging. Even the creeping quackgrass, with its directional line of prostrate roots, was easy to remove as it trailed underneath the cushiony leafy mulch.

The area was so crowded with matured shade plants that to avoid damaging the leaves I had to stand and bend forward at the hips to move between them. Occasionally there was an open space near the base of a tree. Here I could go to my knees and rest my back while the cleanup continued.

I crawled along absentmindedly until a sharp pain went through one knee. I had knelt on a piece of something hard and rounded. Sitting back I rubbed my knee and looked at the spot that had assaulted it. Out of sight under the ferns and hosta leaves was a piece of broken tree limb. It had lain there for some time and was partially rotted with little worm holes running through it. I had knelt on a tough, unyielding edge of the bark.

Usually I leave woodland debris to rest where it has fallen. After all, it's all good stuff nourishing the soil. But this fallen piece of limb was large enough and close enough to the plants that it was forcing them to twist, deforming them as they tried to grow around it. I decided to pick up the limb and break it apart into the compost heap.

Lifting it to one side I saw a scurry of activity. A few brightly-colored bugs darted in multiple directions looping back on themselves, blinded by the unexpected light. They had formed a lace-like pattern in the soil under their familiar roof. Even the back of the cinnamon-colored bark had a lovely silvery pattern reflective of their living trails.

The discovery of the beautiful golden-striped bugs hidden beneath a decaying piece of wood made me smile. Their industrious munching while working in the dark had left delicately curved channels. Usually no one would see and appreciate their usefulness in breaking down pieces of broken limbs. But there they were, simply doing exactly what they had been created to do, lovely in their own peculiar way, as part of the Creator's design to be useful, beneficial, and hidden.

"[Study] and aspire to live a tranquil life, to mind your own affairs and to work with your own hands…"

(1 Thessalonians 4:11)

Thursday: The Scent of Earth

It was the second week of March and I was driving along a country road with my windows down. It had been a freakishly warm and dry winter, setting record highs throughout most of the Midwest. I live in southern Michigan where we've experienced January temperatures in the mid-fifties when they are usually in the lower twenties. February and March followed suit with a number of days running above average.

Heading home with groceries I decided to take the scenic route instead of the highway. The surrounding area is rural with pockets of dairy farms, and fields of wheat, silage and corn. One of the nice things about rural routes is the ninety-degree intersections. No matter how I zigzag across counties I'm confident of finding my way home by heading south and east.

Coming around an S-curve on a two-lane gravel road I saw a farmer taking advantage of the extended and unseasonably mild weather by chisel plowing his field (sometimes incorrectly called disking). Being from Detroit, I am always impressed by the sheer mass of farm machinery and have had to learn its vocabulary: tractors vs. combines, harvesters vs. windrowers, and the finer points of Duals. The familiar green and yellow equipment in the bright spring sun stood out sharply against the dark brown fields.

I remember as a pre-teen I worked on a family friend's farm for part of a summer. Getting up close and personal with farming life was exhilarating and exhausting. When I first arrived I followed the three daughters around the farm to become familiar with our chores. I was awestruck that tractor tires were twice my height, cows lined up all by themselves for milking, and hay bales were relatively light. Although those same hay bales got a lot heavier when we had to stack them on the wagon while out in the field!

I could see the farmer in the cab as he approached the road and, anticipating his turning the equipment, waited and then waved my arm out the window. He smiled, waving back. I saw he was a young man and not like the grizzled gray-haired farmers I was accustomed to seeing.

As we passed each other the barely visible plume of dust from the plowing crossed the road. I was caught by surprise at the enveloping scent of fresh soil. The earth, dark and rich with life, with its damp, heady fragrance drawn fully into my lungs, awoke my senses and made my heart beat faster with a familiar joy. A joy I'm sure that young farmer experienced as well.

The deep smell of earth, like the charged and fragrant air of an approaching thunderstorm, stirs us mysteriously in our core. Eventually we come to recognize, or possibly remember from before our birth, that these are the Scent of God.

Precious Lord,

When I forget you are near, let me recall the words of St. Francis de Sales and place myself in your presence: Help me to know that you are all around me in all things, that you are fully in me and your Holy Spirit is diffused throughout my whole body, and that you my God are affectionately gazing at me at all times.

Amen.

Friday: Pine Cones

I look at the pattern on the top of a pine cone and am fascinated by its rhythmically increasing woody scales. I notice the identical unfurling symmetry of fiddleheads to the shuttlecock ferns under the old apple tree. A few steps away I take a closer look at the sweet woodruff and its whorled leaves clasping the stem, perfectly and evenly spaced. I am in awe and wonder at the measured patterning of creation.

Standing there in the not-yet-shaded area of my garden I remember undergraduate years and all the mathematics requirements. It was a challenge for me to make sense of equations and story problems that involved angles, gradients, percentages and tangential increases; physics too was my nemesis. Somehow I learned it all and succeeded at passing Calculus 2.

I remember one particularly erratic trigonometry professor who had thick wire-rimmed glasses and a full beard. To complete the look of insanity, seriously unkempt bushy black hair puddled on his shoulders. He told us one day in class that he couldn't look anywhere without numbers, angles, and formulas clouding his vision. Equations squiggled nearly transparent behind moving busses; tension formulas danced above telephone poles. And you couldn't even mention to him about a car spinning out of control unless you wanted to hear again the mathematics of deviation amplifying loops! I wondered back then if this irregular kind of guy saw his mathematics as a god. Or did he really believe what he said, that "God is in the numbers"?

Returning to the present, I look again at the top of the pine cone held in my hand. I never expected to find arithmetic in my garden. I think I now understand more fully the unstable professor's insight of God in mathematical formulas, in the amazing grace of rhythm, symmetry, and incremental patterns of growth.

When we look at our spiritual insights, one upon another like the scales of the pine cone, we will see the same tiny incremental increases widening out in a beautiful pattern of a developing holy life. There needs to be a steady pace of learning about Jesus and about the three theological virtues of faith, hope, and love. Then we must live what we've learned as we unfurl and open up to become who we are meant to be. God may indeed be in the numbers…the number of times we seek Him in prayer and friendship, in contemplation, and in the Eucharist.

"All of us gazing with unveiled faces on the glory of the Lord, are being transformed into the same image from glory to glory…"

(2 Corinthians 3:18)

Saturday: Debris

My plan, instead of taking a nap, was to start cleaning up yard waste left by the winter winds and snow. The frigid bite in the air caught in my chest as I walked across the yard. It was the end of March, I fretted to myself, and temperatures by mid-day should have been at least above freezing!

Opening the shed doors, I was faced with a tangled wall of garden ornaments, tools, and furniture stacked six feet high. I made a mental note to buy a second storage shed, and then calculated which items to remove in what order to access the blue Rubbermaid dump wagon at the bottom. My Jenga-playing skills came in handy as the snarl of items found their way onto the drive. When I looked behind me I realized that I would never remember by the end of the day how to put it all back.

With the wagon excavated, and appropriate tools placed inside, I pulled the hood of my sweatshirt up over my head and moved to the west garden, putting on a second pair of brown jersey gloves for warmth. Carefully I picked up debris from the flowerbeds so as not to damage determined hyacinths pushing through partially frozen soil. I snapped off old stems of mums and cut to the ground the ornamental grasses. Moving to the cement driveway, I raked up the circle of straw that afforded my little dog a place of relief when the snow piled higher than she was tall.

In the middle of the drive was a fire pit with last fall's trimmings. Before I ignited the debris I grabbed the branches near the bottom, pulled them up the side and gave them a vigorous shake to free any birds or critters that might be nesting within. Two fat black field mice groggily jumped free and hop-skipped to the tarp-covered gas grill to hide. I deposited my gatherings from the afternoon and began laying them on top to burn.

The fire grew rapidly as scent and smoke rose. I added more fodder for the flames and became aware that under my hoodie goose bumps were forming as the sudden change in temperature warmed me.

I was reminded of the spiritual goose bumps I get at the Easter Vigil. At sunset, the priest in golden vestments stands before a cauldron of fire at the top of the steps and lights the Pascal candle from its flames. I always have the sensation of being spiritually warmed when in the darkened church the single Pascal flame enters the nave, and the light, candle by candle, moves across the pews slowly progressing to the sanctuary.

Standing in the drive I tossed onto the fire a fairly large branch from an arborvitae and was amazed by the sound from the scale-like leaves burning...a sharp tinkling sound like splashing water.

Fire and water are familiar symbols of a life in Christ, the illuminating fire of the Holy Spirit and the baptismal water of new birth. On this cold spring day I felt a baptism and confirmation of sorts, a harbinger of the Vigil to come.

"We are indeed buried with Him by baptism into death so that just as Christ was raised from the dead by the glory of the Father, even so we also should walk in the newness of life."

(Romans 6:4)

Fourth Sunday of Lent: Clouds

It was that time of year when autumn clouds fill the sky for most of a day. They were thick and dense, brilliant white with melding shades of gray.

I love how clouds reflect all the spectrum of light from the sun. Light is made up of the colors of the rainbow, and when all the colors are present in equal amounts you get white.

I wrote in my first book, *A Garden of Visible Prayer*, "White is the color of the Holy Spirit, of truth and sanctity. It represents purity, innocence, and kindness. I read somewhere that white teaches us about relationships because, in our perceptions of colors, it tints how we see. White is in itself not a color but the complete revealed energy (manifestation) of all the colors. A very nice explanation of the completeness of the Holy Spirit." And like the presence of the Holy Spirit that brings light and lightness to my soul, clouds also give me a sense of being weightless.

It is not unusual to see clouds formed at different heights in the stratosphere. When this happens the clouds will appear to move at different speeds relative to their distance from earth. Watching the clouds late one afternoon I saw that this layering had taken place; there were higher Cirrocumulus clouds over heavier Stratus.

What was unusual is that these clouds were running in different directions, clearly moving perpendicular to each other! The higher, whiter clouds were moving due north and the rain-filled Stratus clouds, seeming so low one could almost touch them, sped east and slightly south.

I had never seen this before and stood in the field turning in circles to view all of the sky, eventually sitting against a fence post in awe. My love and learning of natural sciences from undergraduate years began formulating the why of stratospheric wind directions and the collective weight of water vapors. Still, the wonder of the event kept me spellbound for nearly half an hour watching the clouds move.

Later as I reflected upon the event, I came to understand more fully how the currents in our own lives can often run contrary, or perpendicular, to one another. We can seem to be floating along bright and white and above all earthly things, and then lower dark clouds move in and draw our attention down and on a completely different course.

We may need to be attentive to the potential of storms from these lower obscuring clouds. But let us remain focused on the higher clouds in our lives, those that capture the whiteness of The Light and reveal the currents of the Holy Spirit manifest and moving within our souls.

"We must experience our relationship with God between the poles of distance and closeness. By closeness we are strengthened, by distance we are put to the test."

~Pope Benedict XVI

Fourth Week of Lent

Set Free

Remember feeling the physical sensation of liberation? Like at the end of a work day when you take off that shirt that is a bit too snug and slip into a soft cozy sweatshirt two sizes too big? Or maybe it's loosening your belt after a filling meal and leaning into the cushions of the sofa. What about emotionally being set free from something that caused you to feel guilt, or when you discover you are deeply loved?

It's a good feeling to be able to relax, to let go. The muscles you didn't know were tensed, the emotions you didn't realize were distracting, are let loose. You can take a deep breath and sigh with relief.

I can imagine when Lazarus came out of the tomb his sisters were rejoicing at the very moment they were awestruck (John 11:38-44). They were immediately freed of their grief and their fear of vulnerability in a future without their brother. Their sigh of relief was undoubtedly mingled with their songs of praise and glory.

I can imagine how the adulterous woman may have felt when Jesus stood by her in the angry mob (John 8:1-11). Her hidden sins were no longer hidden, her emotional scars obvious, and every muscle in her body tensed as she realized her death was imminent. And then she was liberated — physically, emotionally, spiritually — as the crowd dissipated and the Lord looked her in the eye and asked her to sin no more. Imagine that, Jesus looking you right in the eye releasing you from your sins.

That's what this week is about. Whatever is hidden, whatever is binding, whatever is in excess, He will set us free. And how we will sing when we are freed to grow in His love.

Monday: A Hidden Scar

Working the grounds as a volunteer at St. Francis Retreat Center, I receive great joy in making outdoor prayer spaces. There is really nothing elaborate about the gardens on the ninety-five acre site, but it is gratifying to see how well everything is growing and that we are able to offer people a space where they can draw closer to God. Creating gardens in which to pray is my mission, my calling to serve Our Lord, and I am grateful to have found a group of gardeners willing to help with my vision.

Walking down the path through the Stations of the Cross one day, I came to the driveway and followed it past the Director's Perennials Garden. I noticed as I came around the curve to the front of another building that one of the trees had its trunk wrapped. I did not recall any of us performing the task and wandered over to have a look. A few years ago we had planted this tree, a Chinese Elm, because of its resistance to disease and insects, and I was surprised to see its lower trunk covered.

The tree was wound in black plastic, which is a very bad product to tie around any tree. It prevents air flow and holds moisture, creating an environment for infections. I knew the Groundskeeper would never do this and assumed someone unfamiliar with proper tree care may have tried to help. I was less curious about who had done this than why.

My heart sank after I removed the plastic and saw that a four-foot length of bark had been mechanically stripped from the trunk. The force of whatever had happened had even gashed the wood. I assumed the damage might have been caused by the bucket of a tractor when the mulch had been dumped. Whatever the cause, the beautiful young elm was deeply and forever scarred.

I thanked God that whoever had tried to hide the damage had not compounded the problem by slopping paint or tar on the wound. I was also grateful that the wounding had happened fairly recently and that diseases had not begun to grow under the plastic. With my pocket knife I gently trimmed away frayed pieces of bark. Walking over to the spigot, I turned on the water and with the hose began rinsing the injured area, leaving it to heal in the sunlight.

It was a few days later, when I returned to the tree, that I realized how its wounding led me into a deeper understanding of self. When our souls have been wounded and deeply scarred by sin we try to hide it, often making the situation worse through other wrong choices. Once we accept what has happened and expose the mistake to the Light, we too will be able to heal.

"If you happen to do something that you regret, be neither astonished nor upset, but having acknowledged your failing, humble yourself quietly before God and try to regain your gentle composure. Say to yourself: 'There, we have made a mistake, but let's go on now and be more careful.' Every time you fall, do the same."

~St. Francis de Sales

Tuesday: Chorus of Birds

It was about 3:45 in the morning and I was wide awake. There was nothing wrong, and yet I couldn't sleep. I surrendered to the temporary insomnia and headed downstairs, shadowed by two kitties and an old groggy dog. The house was quiet as I turned on the small fluorescent light over the sink. I pulled the canister of gourmet coffee, a thoughtful gift from a friend, from the back of the counter. After starting the coffee to brew, I walked to the back door and switched on the yard light, being sure to scan the outdoors for wildlife before I let the dog head out for the lawn.

With an oversized cup of freshly brewed Italian Roast, I headed back up the stairs to the prayer room, leaving one kitty curled up in the pet-bed under the kitchen table. Opening the windows a bit further I heard the peeper frogs' soft chirping from a distant pond. Setting the cup on the end table, I settled back in the recliner with the graying little dog curling up between my feet and a long haired-silver cat on my lap. Neither of them was any too happy about my early morning wanderings.

Picking up my rosary, a soft-blue and white millefiori from Rome, I began my usual morning-prayer routine. I've found that there is an unclouded comfort in starting each day drinking a cup of coffee with Christ and his Mother. I'm not one to wake up easily or quickly and this hour with them eases me into the day…one of the special privileges of living a single life.

As that night progressed into morning, before there was even a glimmer of light, I heard a single cardinal let out a tentative whistle; it was 4:08 AM. A few minutes passed and he whistled again, two notes. A similar response emerged from one of the neighbors' trees, and the two birds repeated as their little voices gained confidence.

Like tiny roosters they seemed to be waking the other birds to the coming dawn. Gradually I heard the toning of the robins, the clear trilling of wrens, the beeping of nuthatches, the distinct chirp of chickadees; and finally pitching in were the jays, grackles, red-winged black-birds, and woodpeckers. It was a slow and steady rise like the sunlight, reaching a vibrant morning crescendo. I delighted in their chorus forming a singular proclamation.

I was so caught up in their rising song that I forgot that I was in the middle of a rosary. And yet my song was rising with their voices. My song of prayer, my waking to The Light, blended with their welcoming the dawn.

I wonder if God hears our prayers as I heard the songs of these morning birds. At first a small single tentative voice, waking to new light. As more prayers form, that voice gains confidence, clarity, diversity, and strength. We voice a lively warbling from the melody in our souls. I wonder if God too delights in our boisterous crescendo of songs.

"Fill us at daybreak with your kindness, that we may shout for joy and gladness all our days...prosper the works of our hands, O Lord."

(Psalms 90:14-17)

Wednesday: Releasing Constriction

The beautiful ten-foot Colorado Blue Spruce suddenly took a turn for the worse. Something was killing it and the Groundskeeper asked me to have a look.

The usual causes of sickness had been eliminated. The soil was tested, the fertilizer checked, the watering evaluated, and the common pests researched. Whatever herculean effort was extended to find a cure was minimally effective and at times the decline appeared to accelerate.

As I scooched on my side under the boughs I noticed the tell-tale sign of a narrow bulge around the base of the trunk. Removing the outer layer of mulch and pulling back the ground cloth, I confirmed my suspicion. A piece of hemp rope from the root-ball support was wrapped around the trunk. The rope had not been cut free when the spruce was planted several years ago. The tree had been girdled.

To kill a tree or shrub doesn't take a lot of effort or chemicals. It is a rather simple task, one that a mouse can complete in a matter of hours by chewing through the bark in a ring around the trunk. This damage to the vascular system stops the flow of nourishment from tree to root, and starvation is imminent.

A more frequent form of girdling is caused by carelessness. I have seen it too often. Hardwoods added in the landscape years earlier show sudden signs of decline. Often it is the crown or a major branch, and sometimes, as with the Blue Spruce, the whole tree is affected.

This type of girdling is a result of something barely noticeable. Someone might leave behind a nylon string, wire, or plastic band on a branch when removing a tag. Or, as was the case with the Blue Spruce, a person might forget to unwind the rope from the trunk. As the trunk or branch grows and increases in circumference, the cord left behind will strangle this otherwise healthy specimen.

I think of how careless words can girdle the hearts of children, as when they are made to feel insignificant or worthless. A simple phrase spoken with meanness can stunt a portion of their development. When the same harsh words are repeatedly spoken they twist into an invisible rope that destroys what used to be a sound and vibrant being.

A fortunate few seek to find the mental constriction. When they discover the forgotten band or twisted rope of words that had lain hidden for years, the un-girdling of their hearts is liberating. The binding is removed and, if not too late, nourishment once again flows, slowly at first and often with fits and starts.

On an injured tree or shrub a scar will always remain where constriction has occurred, becoming less pronounced as healing takes place. If the damage is deep and nourishment blocked for too long, thriving may never be an option. So too with us.

I scan the landscape of my soul to spot the tell-tale signs of constriction. I do what I can to promote healing, even if it is simply to pray. The first step is to pull away the debris.

Loving Father,

Help me to embrace my imperfections so that I may be guided in humility and patience. Lead me, Lord, to find the wounds that have remained hidden and release me from their mental constriction. Help me to break these ties that bind my soul and keep me from growing fully in your love. Help me to be confident that though my attempts to be fruitful may fall short, You see the success in my efforts to love.

Amen.

Thursday: Leaves in the Rain

A low rumble of thunder woke me. The weather station had correctly predicted rain by 6:00 AM. Tossing back the summer quilt and sitting up on the edge of the bed, I listened to the morning rainfall starting to *plink* on the metal awnings. I threaded my arms through the sleeves of my robe, noting how the dampness had made my joints markedly stiffer.

A little later, with my usual cup of coffee in hand, I ambled to the upholstered chair, set the coffee aside and slid open both windows. The fresh, cool air caused the sheer white curtains to billow as it entered the house. The raindrops produced a heavy whispering sound as they landed on the leaves of the old apple tree. The aged Northern Spy's distorted limbs passed so near to my second story window that I could easily reach out and shake them.

The apple tree's foliage seemed to dance as big drops of rain splattered heavily against its parched and upturned leaves. The rainwater gained momentum as it moved in small rivulets down the outer tips of the limbs to the leaves below.

There were a lot of leaves on that old tree. The ones toward the center were less soiled and reflected a richer green. Those innermost leaves received the rain too, but shimmied little from the increasing downpour.

The tree was not far from the road so all of the leaves were sullied. The leaves that were dirtiest, in more need of the cleansing rain, were at the outer edge of the limbs. They were more exposed, less sheltered—or cloistered—by the tree's protective canopy. They were also the ones that danced the most as they were made clean.

Something inside me stirred as I watched the purification of the dusty leaves. There was a familiar parable occurring outside the window. All of our souls need cleansing—those that are exposed and those that are cloistered. All of us need to be refreshed by washing away transgressions. The soul dances with the cleansing of Confession, its reconciliation to God.

"Purge me with hyssop, and I shall be clean; wash me, and I shall be whiter than snow. Fill me with joy and gladness...Hide Thy face from my sins, and blot out all my iniquities. Create in me a clean heart, O God, and put a new and right spirit within me."

(Psalms 51:7-10)

Friday: In Excess

There had been an overabundance of rain that spring. Storms, some severe, had scoured the gardens with record amounts of rainfall. And the gardens had not responded well.

Numerous weeds had sprouted, taken root, and become massive in record time. With my inability to remove them between storms, they had thrived with all the moisture. The chickweed, bedstraw, and henbit had energetically blanketed the garden between the pennycress, marestail, and several grasses. They've all produced a lovely and disheartening weedy array of colors and textures within the perennial beds. They, and the desired garden plants, are weak-stemmed from all the rain and lack of sun. As for the opportunistic mushrooms, they had multiplied exponentially in both number and size.

Other things have grown in the garden besides the herbaceous plants—diseases of all kinds. The molds and mildews, fungus and rots had begun their insidious creeping. Their black pus or white fuzz coatings appeared on stems and leaves faster than I could remove the infected material. No matter how careful my attempts to uproot weeds and remove diseased flower stems, I only seemed to be smearing the decay on other plants and my clothes.

As I tried to clean up the flowerbeds I found myself praying for sunlight and soft breezes to heal the gardens, but what came the next week was also in excess. The temperatures went from being in the fifties and sixties, with the weather overcast and rainy, to ninety degrees and above, with a scorching sun. What had flowered now melted, further multiplying the molds and mildews. Then the gusting winds came, blowing so hard that softened stems and weakened branches collapsed and fell to the ground.

The battle had been lost. The gardens were now a limp mass of decaying leaves and stems, weeds and flowers alike.

All I could do was level the garden and let it begin again. With loppers, rakes, and black plastic bags I began cleaning up with a sigh of resignation.

It had been a spring of disproportion, of extremes and excessiveness. That season I had come to appreciate even more our church's teachings of moderation and the virtue of temperance. I was reminded how an overabundance of anything perceived as good, like rain and sun and air, can eventually cause damage and disease if taken beyond a reasonable balance.

<u>1809</u> *Temperance* is the moral virtue that moderates the attraction of pleasures and provides balance in the use of created goods. It ensures the will's mastery over instincts and keeps desires within the limits of what is honorable. The temperate person directs the sensitive appetites toward what is good and maintains a healthy discretion: "Do not follow your inclination and strength, walking according to the desires of your heart." Temperance is often praised in the Old Testament: "Do not follow your base desires, but restrain your appetites." In the New Testament it is called "moderation" or "sobriety." We ought "to live sober, upright, and godly lives in this world."

<u>2290</u> The virtue of temperance disposes us to *avoid every kind of excess*: the abuse of food, alcohol, tobacco, or medicine…

~Catechism of the Catholic Church

Saturday: A Range of Diversity

I'd been pulling weeds and took note of their diversity, growth pattern, and required habitat to flourish. Some were shallow rooted, prolific, and easy to remove. Others, like the dandelion and common mallow, though fewer, had deep tap roots requiring more time to extricate.

Then there were the pretty little weeds with blue flowers that crept along the ground almost like a lace doily. I noticed that Purple Deadnettle overtakes areas that are rich and fertile. For some species it didn't seem to matter where they grew, being nonselective of light or shade.

I pulled out my weed identification book and found over four hundred listed for my region. I had never realized how many of them were familiar. I started to think about all the parables that told of how we need to weed out sins in our lives, to uproot what is opposed to beauty.

None of those parables seemed to fit the spirituality of my gardening this day. It was more about the diversity.

I thought about the pretty little sins, the seemingly innocuous lies that creep into our lives, about how some of our poorer choices run deep and take a great deal of effort to overcome. Those mistakes that we make over and over again are like Quack Grass with its creeping rhizomatous root system—nearly impossible to eradicate, lying hidden just underneath the surface before popping up everywhere. If we deny the pervasiveness of this weed and simply pull at it, it will snap off and grow again. If it remains unattended, it spreads very rapidly, becoming embedded throughout the garden.

The Catechism tells us that, like my weeds, sins are diverse, prone to spread, and can become embedded in the soil of our souls. We read in paragraph <u>1853</u> of the Catechism of the Catholic Church that "Sins can be distinguished according to their objects, as can every human act; or according to the virtues they oppose, by excess or defect; or according to the commandments they violate. They can also be classed according to whether they concern God, neighbor, or oneself; they can be divided into spiritual and carnal sins, or again as sins in thought, word, deed, or omission. The root of sin is in the heart of man, in his free will [...] But in the heart also resides charity, the source of the good and pure works, which sin wounds."

We can see by this reading that there are many ways to hide the beauty of who we are. The root of sin, like the roots of weeds, can conceal the splendor of our gardens.

No matter how careful I am at weeding my garden, it is an ongoing challenge to keep things in check. Being attentive does not mean weeds will not come, only that we can dispatch them more quickly. So true of our souls as well.

Dear Lord,

When I look to the garden that is my soul, I become aware of the habitat in which sin can grow. Help me, Lord, to be mindful of the tangled mess that can result when I am not attentive to the earliest sprouting of sin. Help me to recognize and confess those things that prevent growing fully with your mercy.

Amen.

Fifth Sunday of Lent: Resourcefulness

The little birds chirp and titter, vibrating their wings in greeting to one another and fluttering about unafraid of human presence. Many people call the multitude of sparrows LBBs, short for little brown birds. Where I live we have three different kinds and they are everywhere: in my yard, at the feeder, hopping along sidewalks and at parking lots.

City-dwelling LBBs are very resourceful when it comes to finding food. They'll hop about three feet from where you sit and dart in to grab even the smallest morsel dropped from your lunch. I have watched them from my car as I waited for fast food service, and laughed at their over-burdened flight after nabbing a discarded French fry that was longer than their little bodies.

I am impressed by the cleverness of the LBBs to find food in an area crowded with buildings and covered with cement. One afternoon while walking across the parking lot of a mall, I stopped and delightedly watched the bizarre sight of several LBBs hanging from the grille of a dirty Dodge Ram truck. They were eating dead bugs from the grille! Judging by the number of birds hopping beneath the bumper, impatiently waiting their turn, it was obviously a feast.

The next week in another parking lot, I saw colorful patches of what looked to be crushed chalk with a few of these little birds pecking at it. I thought it odd and rather sad that the LBBs would be so hungry that they would try to eat chalk. That was until I entered through the sliding glass doors to the store and saw on display mini sugar-cookies dyed the same vibrant primary colors.

The LBBs were able to seek nourishment skillfully and promptly no matter how difficult or challenging their situation. They were cautious yet unafraid to look for food in unfamiliar places. Am I at least as courageous as these sparrows in seeking spiritual food?

There are times in all of our lives when we find ourselves surrounded by a world that seems devoid of love, the essential food for our heart and soul. But are we willing to explore new means of nourishment? Are we open to seeking God in unexplored ways? It is easy to become discouraged in times of drought, when all the usual means of sustenance seem to have dried up. I have often sought and received heavenly nourishment through reading scripture, praying the rosary, and attending Adoration and Mass. I have also experienced times when I perceived that these were not enough.

When my heart hungers for God beyond the solitude of prayer, I am often too anxious and shy to move into the world and seek His manna. I become pigeon-hearted and scurry away from any unfamiliar movement no matter how tempting the food.

Maybe I need to pray to be like those little brown birds, with courage to seek, caution in trying, and persistence in my quest to find what will nourish and give me strength for the day.

"He satisfied the longing soul, and filled the hungry soul with goodness."

(Psalms 107:9)

Fifth Week of Lent to Palm Sunday of the Passion of the Lord

Storms

Storms come to everyone. There are the usual storms that move in and eventually depart. But sometimes there are storms of such magnitude you feel as if all will be lost and there is nothing to do but watch. You can be pretty well assured that the apostles thought all was lost when Jesus was arrested. The hardest day and the greatest love story in the history of the world were about to take place, and emotions were running rampant.

When a devastating event slams into our lives it is a challenge emotionally to maintain a view of the bigger picture. We tend to narrow our focus on an issue and in so doing come to rely on ourselves instead of God. We can become defensive when threatened, lose faith as we lose control, and harden our hearts against those who have made our world seem unsafe. We tend to step away from Christ at the very moment we need to draw near, when we are wounded or broken.

There was a lot of stepping away from Jesus as the storm of hatred swirled into its climax during The Passion. On that day there was doubt among the apostles, and deep sorrow for those around the suffering Christ. Many doubted that a man beaten and bloodied unto death would come back to life. It was an absurd statement, as challenging a claim as eating his flesh and blood; the apostles showed a temporary failure of faith in the Eucharist and Resurrection.

We are human and we will doubt...and we will also seek. This is God's design at our creation. For from that seed of doubt we choose to go in search of Him who brings reason to our lives, drawing life from His roots to weather whatever storms may come.

Monday: Soil Compaction

A client's hundred-acre site has multiple soil types within the property, from sandy loam to silty clay and everything in between, including a swamp and a sand berm outcropping. I think about the earth underfoot, about the microbes and all that is invisible to us that make the miracle of soil a thing able to sustain life.

There is wonder and amazement when I think about the soils of the earth. There are desert sands, rich bogs, nutrient-filled clay, mysteriously dark topsoil, stagnant swamps, and frozen tundra, just to name a few.

I think about my own interior landscape and its regions of soils, a topography that is as vast and undulating as that of the earth. The analogies and parables about soil are many, familiar, and worn. We have heard the expressions about the Good Earth, barren soil, and the four soils of the sower in the Bible. There is another soil condition that is rarely considered when drawing on spirituality. It occurs from excessive and recurring pressure, when all that is good and viable is pushed down. It is called compaction.

Compaction is a condition farmers do their utmost to avoid, but it can result if they do not attend to their fields properly. By working the earth too soon in the spring when the soil is wet, too frozen, or too "tender" to be tilled, the weight of the machinery compresses the soil below the surface. Of all agricultural situations, this is the most damaging to sustainability. Water and plant roots cannot penetrate the compressed soil. The field has lost its *tilth*, or its ability to support plant life. The microbes, worms, and all the bugs and bacteria that enliven and sustain the soil are no longer able to penetrate it.

Severe compaction is a parched and barren piece of earth that no amount of tilling or amending with fertilizers can restore to support life. The very essence of its structure, at a molecular level, is beyond recovery. It can only be dug out, ground up, and tossed aside.

This analogy holds true for many individuals whose hearts have become hardened. Their interior soil that should grow loving relationships has been destroyed. On their own without God, no amount of tilling and working will bring their hearts back to His intended purpose. Their hearts are impenetrable to all that is good, though goodness surrounds them on all sides.

Although they cannot return to a loving and full life on their own, God can still enter their hardened, compacted hearts with slow and gentle persistence. Think of rain. A downpour on compacted soil will do nothing except run off and dampen only the top few millimeters. Puddles form on the hard, resistant surface and there evaporate, having never reached the interior.

But a delicate, persistent rain on compacted soil, impenetrable as that soil may be, will penetrate. Gentle rain, like truth, sinks in and softens slowly. Once a heart is softened like the soil, God can begin to rectify the damage.

"O miserable mind of men! O blind hearts! In what darkness of life, in what great dangers you spend this little span of years!"

~Lucretius

Tuesday: Wider Focus

Depression is a state in which hopelessness prevails, where a deep sadness can't be shaken. People feel despondent and inadequate; they lack energy and have difficulty maintaining concentration or interest in life. There are many reasons people struggle with this darkness: a traumatic event in the past, an inability to manage themselves in a present situation, or a chemical imbalance brought on by stress. Severe depression can create a sense that there is no way out, and this perceived narrowing of options contributes further to the depressed individuals' profound despair. Depression is grounded in a sense of purposelessness.

Like many other people, I have struggled with depression. My world became dark and narrowed. I doubted myself and in doubting, my faith began to slip away. I was despairing and couldn't see My Lord. The storm of depression swirled like a contracting funnel cloud, soon to be a tornado.

Initially I didn't recognize the warning signs. My vision was myopic as I focused on getting out of bed, getting through work, and even just breathing. On my own I was not able to find what kept me from the peace I needed. Finally I sought a therapist who shared my Catholic beliefs and might help me reignite my faith.

We had worked together for a while and on this day our session was challenging and seemed particularly long. We covered a lot and attempted to incorporate concepts from previous appointments. I was discouraged and believed I had lost momentum in the healing process. I felt drained, more so than usual, and was eager to return home.

It was a warm August day and the heat seemed as oppressive as my thoughts. It took effort, but I decided to go outside and wander about the gardens. Focusing on spent flowers, I deadheaded by hand as I walked, tossing the exhausted seed heads to the ground.

I heard a clear sharp trilling and looked up. I didn't recognize the high sweet melody of the bird that was on the other side of the yard. I scanned the area from where I thought the sound had come.

The bird sent out another set of notes from the direction of the lilac bushes. My eyes kept trying to pinpoint where the bird was, but I simply could not see it. Again, it trilled its lovely song and again I scanned the lilac, to no avail. I was focusing intensely in one spot, sure the bird was there.

Then it came to me — on several different levels — that if I widened my field of vision I would see movement. I realized how this applied to today's therapy. From the first session onward, there had been incremental advancements toward healing. I did not recognize the progression because I was only concentrating on the issues.

I also saw that this was true with my faith. My limited perspective was met by God's panoramic view. Once I stopped trying to focus on one small area, a snapshot in time, then I would see the movement of God in my life and the movement of my life toward God.

I took a slow, deep breath, calmly stood up straight, and relaxed my focus. As my field of view widened to encompass what was in front of me, sure enough, movement became apparent.

"By waiting and by calm you shall be saved, in quiet and in trust..."

(Isaiah 30:15)

Wednesday: Fallen and Flowering

Agitated and emotionally drained, I needed the calming effect of a drive through the country. Riding in a car allows me to displace present and persisting mental challenges, and gives me a sense of "being away."

I headed north on a blacktopped two-lane road. It was late morning and the clouds' shadows were clearly defined. I watched them move across the fields and up the sides of bordering wind breaks and wood lots.

The road pointed straight to the distant horizon, no curves or hills. I passed farms and fields, homes and trees without notice or care. The low rumble of the car's tires was soothing. Like a clothes dryer to babies or white noise for the sleepless, the rhythmic drone dulled my senses.

I had been on the road awhile when up ahead I saw a flowering white tree growing on a ditch-line slope. Its shape was odd and from a distance I mistook it for a very large shrub. As I neared I saw the tree had been broken in two. The sight of a tree split in half is not uncommon, but to see one split like this and flowering profusely was a reason to stop.

The shattered tree had not fully matured, but was still a good size. The trunk was split right down the center and half of the tree rested on the ground. What catastrophic event had assaulted it? What had broken it to its core, leaving it forever contorted? I parked the car. I wanted to touch this tree.

I walked into the ditch and looked up the incline. I had a clear view of the tree's trunk. The side closest to the road was smooth and had a silvery sheen. The center gash had large slices of exposed wood fanning out and connecting the twisted, grounded portion. I tried to determine if it had been snow and ice that caused the break, or maybe lightning or a wind sheer. I decided it didn't matter what had caused the damage; it was a wonder the tree had lived at all.

The leaves on both halves were shiny and fully developed. I thought that there would be some distortion to their growth, at least on the damaged side. The prolific flowers were fragrant and newly opened. I could hear the buzzing of excited bees as they whirled, dizzily gathering pollen. By the looks of it, the tree would bear fruit and feed the community of birds or any number of wildlife.

Taking a few steps toward the tree I bent down under the flowering limbs and closer to its scarred frame. The wound was old, partially healed over and not as ugly with infection as I thought it would be. I was tentative about placing my hand—first just my fingertips, and then my palm—against the smooth bark, but felt emotionally lighter after having touched the tree's disfigured trunk.

The tree's life had been shortened by the wounding; the damage had caused unexpected stress to its growth. Standing before that tree I was in awe because, though severely broken and damaged, it lived, flowered, and bore fruit. I wondered if those of us who have been deeply wounded, and who are working with God to manage our pain, are living examples as beautiful and fruitful as this tree.

"Let the trees find you when you are lost."

~American Blackhawk Indians, *Poetry and Prayers*

Thursday: Empty Nets

I see myself as a gardener, one whose core identity is tied to soil and seeds, and who is happiest when bare feet are touching earth and sod. I am a digger with calloused hands, broken nails, and patched, dirty jeans. I know what to do and what to say and how to interact within the framework of gardens.

But I am increasingly unsure of myself as I am uprooted from what is familiar. The increased discomfort of an arthritic spine, the result of an auto accident decades ago, has forced me to leave the work I have always loved. I can no longer do the physical work needed to maintain gardens and landscapes. In my own yard the daily four to six hours of toiling, weeding, and transplanting is now reduced. I can only work two or three twenty-minute sessions a couple times a week, and I have to avoid strenuous work like digging holes or pruning overhead branches with loppers. I abandoned greenhousing a couple of years ago.

I found it particularly challenging one recent summer to accept my new limitations. My gardens were so neglected that it looked as if no one lived at my house. Tall and rampant lambsquarters and marestail weeds were choking out perennials and shrubs. I was embarrassed by the slovenly appearance of my once pristine yard. Resignation was setting in as I contemplated calling friends to salvage my beloved plants, removing them to their own gardens.

When my mind is busy and wanting action but my body indicates otherwise, it is a challenge to find a balance between being productive while quieting physical discomfort. Like the story of Simon from Luke's Gospel, I keep going out into deep waters looking for a means of livelihood and pull in nothing but empty nets (Luke 5:1-11).

A certain amount of doubt or desperation creeps in when we repeatedly fail to adapt what is familiar to an unknown situation. Just like Simon, we move confidently out on to waters that have always provided for our needs only to find that there is nothing to be had.

It is within this self-doubt that Our Lord comes to us. Even though our failure to succeed was not due to lack of trying, He asks us to try again and leaves it up to us to choose to do as asked. Am I as willing as Simon, who was overworked and exhausted, to venture once again into deep waters? Am I ready to ask those who have gone with me before to this place of empty nets, to come and help again? Am I open to saying, "…we have worked hard…and caught nothing…but at your command I will lower the nets" and trust Jesus to provide?

I wonder what will become of my "Yes, Lord" as I trudge back to that place of non-fulfillment, back to gardens and soils and sod. How will my life change if I too am filled to overflowing with multiple gifts from God? Whose hands will help bring an unexpected bounty to shore?

Maybe my greatest fear isn't the empty net at all, but the full one of success— the full net that redefines who I am as a gardener and the purpose of His gifts.

Merciful and Ever Loving God,

When I turn away from your call to try again, when drifting on a sea that seems empty, when I doubt in a future I cannot fathom, give me strength to trust in Your providential love.

Amen.

Friday: Doubt

On the cover of a July issue of *Magnificat* is a painting of Anne and Joachim, Mary's parents. In looking at this image it occurred to me that there may have been a lot of doubts in this nuclear family.

The elderly Anne and Joachim were childless. Legend tells us that on one particular day the sadness of this situation overwhelmed Joachim. He left the temple and set off to the mountains to be alone with God. He wandered and lamented, doubting he and Anne would ever know the joy of playing with a child of their own.

Anne heard about her husband's tears. As his wife she would have spoken of her barrenness with him, and of her doubt that in their advanced years they would ever have a son or daughter. Anne too went off by herself to pray. Would God answer her plea this time? Would he bring her beloved Joachim down from the mountains and into her empty arms? She doubted that her husband could endure the shame of childlessness much longer.

I can imagine their despair and hope colliding as they prayed. Hopelessness and trust were equally present in their hearts, reality nurturing one and faith the other.

That day God sent an angel to each of them. Anne was told she would conceive and the fruit of her womb would bless the world. A similar promise was made to Joachim. Did an angel really say they would have a child? They each had to see the other to share what they had been told. Falling into each other's arms they knew by the joy in the other's face that a miracle would take place and a child like no other would be born.

Anne bore a daughter and named her Mary. She and Joachim reared their beautiful child with awe and wonder at her grace and ability to grasp the roots of their Jewish faith.

Then one day their daughter, now a young woman, stood before them flushed with apprehension. How could they believe her fanciful story—that she was pregnant, but not by Joseph, her betrothed, not by a man; *that she was impregnated by God?*

This was their daughter and they knew her heart. God had whispered into this child a purity of soul. Very soon Anne and Joachim understood the magnitude of Mary's claim.

Soon Mary's fiancé Joseph learned his betrothed was pregnant. What would he have thought? How could he focus on his work? Imagine that poor man wandering the countryside looking for building materials and stopping to sit under a shade tree weeping about the sexual betrayal of his beloved. If there had been violence against her he would have known. To sleep with another man was an action wholly incongruent with Mary's nature, and yet there was proof. She was with child, and it wasn't his.

Anne and Joachim knew that Joseph needed to believe in a truth that they could not explain. He would have to come to know, on his own terms with God, a truth that never existed before. There was nothing they could say to remove the apprehension in Joseph. But they could give him time to nurture the seed of faith.

During this time Joseph wrestled with his doubts and prayed with an aching and weary heart. In his despair God came to him. God enlightened him of a truth so preposterous and outrageous that only God could have created it. So, too, did Joseph come to understand the magnitude of Mary's claim. Joachim and Anne rejoiced knowing Joseph believed what they had known for months.

All of Mary and Joseph's relatives heard of Jesus. How many of them counted the months from marriage to birth? Did they have faith enough to believe that angels had repeatedly come to Mary and Joseph—that an immense star had appeared at his birth—that Joseph had a premonition to flee to Egypt? Did they later believe the stories of Jesus as a young man who worked miracles?

Not all of the family accepted what they heard. The seeds of doubt grew so much that Jesus was blocked from sharing His gift of healing with them.

If there is anything we can learn from this bit of history, it is that doubt is a part of human nature. We must and will wrestle with it because a seed of doubt is the same size as a seed of faith; the greater growth occurs in whichever seed we nurture. God entrusted us to nurture faith.

"Relieve the troubles of my heart; bring me out of my distress...Let integrity and uprightness preserve me; I wait for you O Lord."

(Psalms 25:17, 21)

Saturday: Held Aloft

At Mass I was hoping to blend in, not wishing to be greeted by fellow parishioners. I didn't want to answer the shallow question of "How are you?" from mere acquaintances. "Fine" was not the honest answer I could give, and the truth was not what they were seeking.

Head down, avoiding eye contact, I slid into a pew near the back of church and, looking at the crucifix, told the Lord that I was sorry for my lack of gratitude and focus. My body ached, my anxiety was picking up speed, and hopelessness was circling like a vulture.

I was not the only one dealing with extended unemployment. I was older, well educated, and with far too much experience for most businesses during these times of economic uncertainty. No one wanted to hire me. I had tried not to take it personally, but it was getting hard.

As I searched for work, I'd exhausted all the benefits I could acquire as a healthy single woman without children, too young for Social Security and Medicare. I was humiliated to be a charity case relying on friends to support me. I was also humbled by their willingness to share what little they had. I tried to remember that it is just as Christian to allow others to give a gift as it is to give one.

Still, I was tired of trying and hoping. I knew I was falling into darkness.

Sitting there surrounded by others in the congregation, I had an image of a leaf falling from the branch of a very tall tree. Initially I thought it was a metaphor of falling away from the tree of my life, tumbling hopelessly detached from all that I knew.

But as I sat there in the quiet with Our Lord, I remembered how a leaf falls, swishing back and forth upon the breeze. It is lifted and carried aloft by the wind, as I too am carried aloft by the breath of God...to eventually be gently grounded.

Jesus, Lord of Heaven and Earth,

I love and adore you. You alone know how unsure I am of my present and my future. You alone, Lord, see the anxiety and darkness that I carry within me. You alone know how confused I am and how often I move and act within my own fear, failing to trust in You.

Send Your light of love into my deepest being. Send me Your courage that I may act clearly and boldly in every situation that challenges my faith in Your will for my good.

I trust in you, Jesus, to carry me aloft when I feel I am falling too fast.

Amen.

Palm Sunday of the Passion of the Lord: Broken Branches

The clouds are moving in quickly, billowing, thunderous, and dark with rain. I can feel the temperature drop significantly as the previously light breeze turns to a gusting wind. The squirrels have disappeared and the birds fallen silent. All these are clear indications that the approaching storm is going to be intense.

I gather the garden tools and head for the shed; the weeds on the lawn can wait until tomorrow. Latching the shed door I head for the house as the first big drops of rain start to fall. My mini-pinscher, Lilly, is dancing on two legs near the kitchen door. She is quite concerned that I will not open it soon enough—she hates getting wet—and makes distressed barks as I walk across the drive.

Hurrying, I begin closing windows and when all are shut, I head out to the screened front porch. Standing there I watch the sheets of rain snake to horizontal from the wind. The mist the rain forms as it drives through the screens dampens my forearms, making the skin draw up into goose bumps.

We have a lot of storms and an occasional tornado in southern Michigan. Mainly the generic types of storms pass through here. They move in steadily, hang around for the expected duration, and then continue their movement eastward. Good rains, nourishing rains.

Then there are *the storms*. Those make my heart beat fast with anticipation and anxiety. For those I stand as near as I dare to the windows and monitor the skies for changes in color, listening for the rain to turn hard and counting the seconds between lightning flashes and the resulting thunder. All the while I'm weighing in my head when it will be necessary to grab the pets and make the run to the basement.

All storms end eventually, and after the big ones there is usually the debris of broken branches littering the street and lawns. The weakest limbs, those that have declined from lack of nourishment, have snapped off during the turbulent downpour. It is usually those branches that had grown farthest away from the trunk that have fallen away.

When sufficient energy is not drawn up from the root, the branch becomes weak and it no longer has enough life within it to withstand the storms. This offers a pretty clear analogy of how I should live: Drawing life from His strong roots, developing a living faith, keeping me strong so I won't break apart in the turbulent storms that come.

<u>162</u> Faith is an entirely free gift that God makes to man [...] To live, grow, and persevere in faith until the end we must nourish it with the word of God; we must beg the Lord to increase our faith; it must be "working through charity," abounding in hope, and rooted in the faith of the Church.

~Catechism of the Catholic Church

Holy Week to Easter Sunday

Germination

It is the holiest week in our Catholic faith, a week of anticipation; we are both anxious about The Passion and eager for His Resurrection. The lesson of trusting in the hidden process of death into life becomes apparent. This week we are brought full circle from Ash Wednesday and reminded that death is transition.

I've always liked the idea of seeds falling to the ground and growing into something amazing. We have read in the Bible since childhood that unless a grain of wheat falls into the earth and dies, it remains just a seed, but if it dies it transitions or germinates, to grow and bear fruit (John 12:24). In horticultural terms, it "dies" from being a seed to being a cotyledon and develops into a fruitful plant. This is the mystery of growth not only for the seeds of plants but for the seeds of faith in our soul as well. Unless those seeds are allowed to germinate, nothing will become of them.

Germination is defined as to begin to grow or develop, to come into existence, to begin. The word comes from Latin, *germinō*, and means sprouted, budded, having put forth. And isn't this what we are called to do with our faith as Christians?

God has planted His seeds within each of us and it is up to us to develop and grow well in the Lord.

Monday: Late Easter

Three weeks had passed since I last I saw the sun. Three weeks of cold hard rains preventing work in the gardens. Three weeks of darkness as I waited for the reawakening of not only my garden but my outlook as well. It had been an unusually challenging Lent as I waited for the resurrection at Easter.

I noticed how that year's lateness of my gardens paralleled the lateness of Easter. The full moon after the vernal equinox was four weeks, placing Easter Sunday a week after that on April 25th. The last time Easter occurred that late was nearly seventy years before, and according to weather archives that too was a cold, late spring.

It was the end of April, when a riot of color from hardy bulbs and flowering shrubs should be adorning the landscape. Not much was showing but hyacinths, daffodils, and forsythia — the declaration of spring that should have come in March. The tulip leaves had only recently unfurled; their blooms, small green triangles layered one against another, were still tucked deep inside. Even the bulbous iris and tiny blue muscari were holding tight their buds.

Mother's Day, which would be in less than two weeks, had always been heralded with the fragrance of lilacs. I love lilacs; their cone-shaped flowers fill the air with aromatic joy. In my garden there are four lilac cultivars, each a different color: double periwinkle, white stripes on dark magenta, a nodding delicate pink from my great-grandmother's yard, and the single lavender shared in common with most of my neighbors.

I walked back from the mailbox and stopped to look at the nearly naked lavender lilac and pulled down a branch for closer inspection. I could tell that the lilacs too were late; most of the flowering buds barely formed. The lilacs might be leafed out by Mother's Day, and if we warmed up enough in the next ten days, a few blooms might open. Disappointed, I let the limb snap back. I needed the lightness of spring's aromas and colors to lift my languid spirit.

I felt a lateness or maybe a lowness in my heart. I knew deep inside there was a season of spring waiting to arise. It was growing, hidden in darkness like the bulbs in my garden. Those bulbs needed the darkness and also rain, but this year there seemed to be an overabundance of both. They too were waiting for sunlight and warmth to flower.

We all face times of weariness. I am challenged to keep faith that God is watching over me. There have been a lot of changes in my life, events I couldn't control that were both humbling and humiliating. Resulting from these changes are new situations taking me far beyond my comfort zone. Intellectually I know I am blessed; emotionally and spiritually all seems dim.

I am called to wait—to be patient and see what will arise from what has been planted inside me, a gardener. I am called to trust in the invisible process of growth. I pray that what is hidden from me during this season of Lent will leaf out and break bud with the resurrection of Easter.

Creator of all that grows from seed,
Light of all who are in darkness,
Awaken me, draw me free
To the miracle of growth
—roots, leaves, blossoms—
To the possibilities of a life in you
—soul, body, spirit—
So that I may praise you
In my work, and rest, and play.

Amen.

Tuesday: Spent Daffodils

I sat in silence on the couch beside my dear friend of over twenty years. Across the darkened room from us were sliding glass doors to her deck. The silk flowers from last fall were still standing tall in two large containers near the back. The spring sunlight brought them to life as they glowed their rich orange and yellows, seeming less out of place than they had in late January.

My friend loves gardens and enjoyed the two small patches on each side of the porch at the front of her house. Last year I did my best to keep them up for her as chemotherapy robbed her of her strength. By the end of summer she only saw them as she shuttled to and from a car.

On this weekly visit she was unusually quiet and seemed weak. When I had called earlier in the morning to make sure she would not be at medical appointments she said that she hadn't eaten much in the past two days. We shared doubts about my bringing lunch.

I called a friend who works at a nursing facility and asked what to bring someone that sick with cancer. She made a few suggestions, one of which was potatoes. My dear sick friend loves potatoes. She had told me stories of growing potatoes when she was a girl. Over the years I had shared with her potatoes from my own garden: Pontiac Reds, Yukon Gold, and more recently Kennebec...her favorite.

Early last summer, while she watched, I had planted a few hills of Kennebec in a small raised bed at the corner of her house. Several weeks later when harvested, she ate them almost daily until they were gone.

So on this day, for our lunch, I brought mashed potatoes and gravy from KFC. I brought enough for a single meal, which for her would last several days. She was delighted when I set a small steaming bowl of them on the TV tray before her. I watched her savor each spoonful—there were only five—and then lunch was over.

We continued to sit together as she dozed in and out. I held her hand and looked at how thin and porcelain its skin had become. At one waking moment I asked her, "How goes it with your soul?" She smiled fully, chuckled lightly, and answered, "Just fine." I smiled back and we recognized the joy in each other's eyes. The gift of a life well lived is peace while the body declines. Then a shadow passed over her face and she said that though she wasn't having any trouble with "it" a lot of others around her were. She turned away and looked out the patio doors.

I followed her eyes to where several gaily wrapped and ribboned pots of spent daffodils sat on the steps to the deck. Easter gifts from well-wishers, no doubt. She asked me about planting them for her out in front of the house. I said I would, adding that bulbs forced to flower for spring sales had only a twenty percent chance of surviving until next year.

As she leaned back into the couch I smiled to myself: My dear friend, always hopeful, intended to see them bloom next spring. That was until she whispered, "They have better odds than I."

I patted her hand and we smiled again. I would plant the daffodils next week and in the meantime pray she would be strong enough to come out and supervise the effort. I knew whatever blooms might come, she would enjoy them from heaven.

"Since we are pilgrims, this Incarnate Word has accompanied us on our journey, and has given us Himself as food to enable us to run courageously… When we reach the end in death, he puts us to rest in that bed, that peaceful sea of divine being, where we receive the eternal vision of God."

~St. Catherine of Siena

Wednesday: It's All About the Soil

There is a lot to be said about the quality of the soil in our gardens. I wrote about it briefly in the previous section.

The soil supports all aspects of plant development and vitality. Artificial potting mixes used in greenhouses or plants grown hydroponically in nutrient-rich water only give the appearance of stable development. Proper soil provides structure, nutrients, and a system of interdependence among living organisms for development of strong healthy roots.

A good soil must be loose enough to allow roots to move in and through it. When soil is hard and compressed, the roots are constricted and do not grow properly, often curling back upon themselves in an endless circling. When this happens the roots are said to become girdled; the soil is squeezed out as the root wraps around itself, eventually eliminating its own means of support.

When a soil is too soft or porous, the root will spread quickly and wildly, making multiple thin roots, trying to stabilize itself in a shifting environment. The lack of deep roots often means the plant lacks the proper nutrition it needs to grow.

A thriving plant also needs a community of organisms, which I have termed *earthworks*, that includes worms, bugs, fungi, and other microorganisms. This synergetic society of earthworks is necessary to break down plant waste and garden debris. It is this relational working together that keeps the soil useable and avoids stagnation.

A healthy, supportive root system develops slowly and steadily, often in set stages of growth and rest. One stage of rapid growth is at the initial planting when the existing root system has been disturbed and exposed to a richer environment. The soil is easily incorporated into the new life of the plant as the roots reach into it seeking food. During those times of rest, when visible activity diminishes, the steady development of roots continues in a less demanding and more stabilizing way.

The relationship of our roots in the soil of the Holy is much the same. We need a steady flow of that which feeds us and gives us life. We need a balanced soil to secure our roots, a soil matched to our individual needs — for a bog plant cannot grow in a prairie. We need a community around us to help break down the debris of life and turn it into something useable.

We have all seen it happen. A beautiful plant exposed to the radiance of the sun will wither if it lacks the roots to draw itself upright.

It doesn't matter how much The Light shines on you, or how often you are exposed to the miracle of God. If you do not have good roots, you will have only an appearance of the fullness of life.

<u>1394</u> As bodily nourishment restores lost strength, so the Eucharist strengthens our charity, which tends to be weakened in daily life [...] By Giving himself to us Christ revives our love and enables us to break our disordered attachments to creatures and root ourselves in him...

~Catechism of the Catholic Church

Holy Thursday: Seeds Germinate

The spring retreat I was leading would start in a few hours. At the last minute I decided to make a small gift for the attendees. I took a piece of easily biodegradable paper and wrote a blessing on the outside. Mixing a packet of seeds with a couple of tablespoons of potting mix, I then wrapped a small amount of the seed-soil mix in the paper, tying it all together with garden twine. The attendees would be instructed to bury their blessings in their gardens and wait for what would come into the light.

Most living things experience a passage from darkness to light. Whether it is in the womb of the body or the womb of the earth, germination takes place in the absence of light. A seed is planted in the dark soil, and with minimal effort on our part, it grows.

The miracle of plant seeds is that everything needed for growth is contained within and waiting to be expressed. It is already fertile, has all the DNA needed for living, and is literally hanging in the balance between its current static state and upcoming life. Research has shown that seeds stored in a jar away from light can hang in this balance for decades. Once those seeds come in contact with moist soil they germinate and rapidly seek sunlight.

The size of the seed doesn't matter; they all contain the genetic material needed to give rise to a new plant. From the tiniest, powder-like seeds of an orchid (even smaller than a mustard seed) to the weighty seeds of palms, all are designed to sprout. It is like there is a tiny glow at the center of every seed wanting to get out, a fleck of light seeking light beyond the darkness of the soil in which it was planted.

It is awe-inspiring when we realize that God chose the things of the earth to express Himself to us. From the simplest thing of a garden, the seed, comes the greatest revelation. It is from the grain of wheat and the fruit of grapes that we receive bread and wine, bread to nourish and wine to gladden (Ps. 104:14-15). Both are essential: the bread of life and fruit of the vine, the Body and Blood of Christ—Eucharist. From that tiny light in a seed to the startling Light of God at Communion, we hear at every Mass "light from light."

The Divine Seed, Jesus, like most seeds, germinated in the dark. He germinated in the darkness of Mary's womb, and grew a religion from a blackened tomb in the earth.

We understand darkness. We were born from a place without light, and our earth was formed out of darkness. Much like the seed to which the absence of light is essential to set root and grow, we too have an inner need for darkness. Without the experience of darkness we would not recognize light. Our roots of belief grow in the fact that Jesus rose from the darkness of his Passion. He rose from an earthen tomb. We sprout and develop faith, our light drawn to His light. We bear fruit by being nourished and fed by that which came from the earth—wheat and grapes, bread and wine. And with seeds from the Fruits of the Spirit we plant kernels of goodness and pray that these seeds too will germinate and take root.

"For you were once darkness, but now you are light in the Lord. Live as children of light, for light produces every kind of goodness and righteousness and truth. Try to learn what is pleasing to the Lord."

(Ephesians 5:8-10).

Good Friday: Fast from Sin; Turn to Virtue

If you are reading this about fasting from sin then it is doubtful that you feast upon sinning. More than likely you are like most people that trip and slip into sin with your virtue falling face-first into the mud of life. Yeah...me too.

The thing about sinning that has always left me feeling a bit confused is that I cannot *not* sin. It is after I've messed up that I draw closer to God, and by seeking Him delight Him...but my sinning doesn't delight Him...but I can't not sin...and I try to be virtuous...and...well...on it goes. So I go to confession regularly and try repeatedly to "avoid the near occasion of sin," knowing full well that I will be back in a couple of weeks to reconcile all over again. And God is pleased.

It is when I am focused on God's third-day-creations — water, land, and plants — that sifting through my failures or successes at virtuousness becomes apparent.   There is something about looking at a rampant vine that helps me realize there are multiple influences twisting my actions or inactivity. It is in the quiet of the moment while in prayer that I am able to work backwards from the contorted branching and vining to the root and see the origins of virtue gone astray.

I find too that grubbing in the soil helps to literally unearth what is buried deep within me, things like resentments, unforgiveness of past hurts, and pride. There is a patience needed to working soil, which is especially true with a patch of hardened clay or shifting sand. A hardened part of my heart may take months to soften. A sandy slope of stubborn self-righteousness usually takes longer. As most gardeners know, amending soil isn't a singular effort, nor is amending a soul.

I have always found a comfort in parables that reference nature. Like most people, and especially those who garden or farm, these stories are the easiest to contemplate and apply to our own personal lives. They make it easy to understand how to grow our virtues and ultimately to create "a garden in which our Lord can take His delight."

<u>1803</u> ...A virtue is an habitual and firm disposition to do the good. It allows the person not only to perform good acts, but to give the best of himself. The virtuous person tends toward the good with all his sensory and spiritual powers; he pursues the good and chooses it in concrete actions. The goal of a virtuous life is to become like God.

<u>1804</u> *Human virtues* are firm attitudes, stable dispositions, habitual perfections of intellect and will that govern our actions, order our passions, and guide our conduct according to reason and faith. They make possible ease, self-mastery, and joy in leading a morally good life. The virtuous man is he who freely practices the good. The moral virtues are acquired by human effort. They are the fruit and seed of morally good acts; they dispose all the powers of the human being for communion with divine love.

~Catechism of the Catholic Church

Holy Saturday: Mud Pies

Mud pies are fun to make; they are moist and gravelly, squishing between the fingers and cooling warm hands and arms. Much to my mother's dismay, making mud pies was my favorite way to play by myself on hot summer days.

I had a favorite mud hole between my father's greenhouses and cold-frames. It was a hidden place where the water-line had a slow continuous leak and was partially shaded by multi-trunked weed trees growing within the chain-link fence. A small pile of discarded wood had been pushed in and around the scrubby trees. There were enough of these moss-covered boards so that when I sat on them they came just below my knees. This allowed my toes to squish into the edge of the mud as I leaned between my legs to work the water deeper into the soil.

The mud would soon thicken into a slippery mass as I kneaded it. This particular puddle had just the right amount of clay to hold together the soft, rotting sticks and leaves. I would squish and squeeze the cool muck, sometimes getting squirted as it oozed between my fingers. Then, when the consistency was just right, being smooth and firm, I would create more than just a pie.

I would make little fairy dishes of cups and saucers, and pick moss to place inside the bowls so they looked to be filled with a salad. Sometimes I would form little animals like dogs or mice. My favorite mud creatures to make were turtles. I would draw patterns on their backs, adding tiny pebbles to accentuate the designs. Talking to myself, and to my little creations, whiled away many a childhood afternoon in a delightful self-absorbed way.

I have always believed that God plays and have often wondered about God playing in the mud. He too must have liked playing this way because He took the water and the clay and squished it around to form a person (Gen. 2:7). God being

God, He could have just willed us into existence, according to Sister Mary Martin, but instead shaped us with a potter's hand.

In my childhood mind, God played in the dirt just like me. I'm sure He too made silly things, some of which He brought to life. Funny little sea creatures like the puffer fish, geoduck, or a seahorse. And how did He ever imagine a star-nosed mole or a platypus?

God delighted in creating, in gardens and growing things, and in sharing what He made. He made us in his own image and instilled in us ways to be joyful, and that includes silliness too.

"The heavens declare the glory of God; the firmament proclaims the works of his hands."

(Psalms 19:2)

Easter Sunday: Extravagance

It's been a journey of sowing seeds and of being sown. I feel the seeding within myself as God's small hard fruits land and take hold in the soil of my soul. This sowing is not new. He has repeatedly scattered seeds with reckless abandon upon the landscape of my heart. On all the different terrains with deep or shallow soils, among my weeds and along His path, often divergent to my own, He has broadcast His grain.

And then He waited. God can afford to be extravagant with sowing seeds.

Compassionate Lord,

How often have we tried to hide ourselves from your bright and exposing light? It is often more comfortable to believe that we are protected by keeping things hidden. Once we see our actions revealed in the light of truth, try as we might we cannot reclaim their perceived comfort.

Your brightness and truth bring an uncomfortable recognition of our personal deceit and vulnerability. We ask you, Lord, to have mercy and guide us to self-awareness that we may be filled with your love and that we may share this love with others.

Amen.

About the Author

Margaret Rose Realy, Obl. O.S.B., has a master's degree in Communications from Michigan State University and is the author of *A Garden of Visible Prayer: Creating a Personal Sacred Space One Step at a Time*. She is an Advanced Master Gardener with thirty-five years of experience as a greenhouse grower, garden consultant, and workshop leader. She is a monthly columnist at CatholicMom.com and blogs about gardening and spirituality at Patheos.com.

CPSIA information can be obtained at www.ICGtesting.com
Printed in the USA
LVOW13s2228260214

375280LV00005B/581/P